Woman, Why Do You Weep?

Asma El Dareer

For All Women

Woman, Why Do You Weep?

Circumcision and Its Consequences

Asma El Dareer

Zed Press, 57 Caledonian Road, London N1 9DN

Woman, Why Do You Weep? was first published by
Zed Press, 57 Caledonian Road, London N1 9DN.

Copyright © Asma El Dareer, 1982

Copyedited by Anna Gourlay
Proofread by Anna Gourlay
Cover design by Jan Brown
Cover photo courtesy of Anne Cloudsley
Typeset by Lynn Papworth
Printed by Krips Repro, Meppel, Holland

British Library Cataloguing in Publication Data
Dareer, Asma El
  Woman, why do you weep?
  1. Infibulation
  I. Title
  618.8   GN481
  ISBN 0-86232-098-4
  ISBN 0-86232-099-2 Pbk

U.S. Distributor
Lawrence Hill & Co., 520 Riverside Avenue,
Westport, Conn. 06880, U.S.A.

Contents

Tables

Acknowledgements

I would like to thank those individuals and organizations whose advice and financial support enabled me to conduct my research, analyse the data and write up the results of this project. I am deeply grateful to the World Health Organization which initiated this project; and my thanks, too, go to the Faculty of Medicine in Khartoum, the Sudanese Ministry of Health, the International Planned Parenthood Federation, and the Ministry of Foreign Affairs, Netherlands; all of whom provided money for the project.

My gratitude also goes to Dr Yahia Own Alla and Dr Siddiq Mohammed Ahmed, and to Dr Suliman Mudawi, Dr Bashir Hamad and Dr A/Gaffer Mohammed Ahmed for their invaluable help and guidance in designing the questionnaires.

Thanks, too, to all the members of the field team who shared in collecting the data and to the computer staff who analysed it. I also thank the Minority Rights Group, Mrs Lilian Sanderson, Judy El-Bashra and Judy El-Nager.

And finally, my utmost gratitude and love to my family and all who shared my problems.

Asma El Dareer

Introduction

I was circumcised in 1960, at the age of 11 years. I remember
every detail of that operation, and that the worst part was when
the wound became infected and I had to be given five injections
of penicillin by the operator, a qualified nurse. From that time
I began to think, to wonder why girls are circumcised and to learn
more about it.

When I was 18 years old it was the turn of my younger sister
to be circumcised, I was totally against her circumcision. My
father wanted the sunna type for her but my mother insisted on
the pharaonic type; eventually my sister had the extreme stage of
the intermediate type, i.e., virtually the same as pharaonic. I still
vividly remember how for seven days she cried and complained of
painful and burning micturition. All the time I kept telling my
mother of the terrible effects of this custom, which she could see
for herself. The suffering of my sister made me hate circumcision
even more than my own, earlier experience.

Circumcision of women was practiced in Ancient Egypt, as the
evidence of female mummys from 200 BC has demonstrated. In
the Sudan, and several other developing countries, the circumcision
of women is quite common. Over 90% of the women are circumcised in the Northern part of Sudan, which is inhabited by 75% of
the total population of the country; to varying degrees, the
inhabitants are of mixed Arab descent — mainly Muslims. In the
South there are some Christians and Muslims, but most of the
inhabitants practice their own traditional religions. Circumcision
is not performed among the indigenous inhabitants except in some
cases where they come into contact with northerners, by marriage
or as neighbours.

The operation is usually performed when a child is four to eight
years old but sometimes as early as seven days old. The result

almost invariably causes immediate and long term medical complications, especially at childbirth. Consummation of marriage is always a difficult experience for both partners, and marital problems often result. Psychological disturbances in girls due to circumcision are not uncommon.

Female circumcision in the Sudan was first seen as a social problem in the late 1930s, when it was widely discussed by the British administration and enlightened Sudanese. The majority of educated Sudanese felt that it was the duty of their generation to abolish this custom. In 1946, the Legislative Assembly passed a law making Pharaonic circumcision an offence punishable by fine and imprisonment. (The sunna circumcision was considered to be legal). This measure, however, proved to be a failure.

As a fifth-year medical student, I found an opportunity to learn more about this practice. As part of the course in Community Medicine we were required to undertake a research project. Without hesitation I chose the subject of female circumcision. From my research for this project I discovered that this custom continued to be practiced only for traditional and religious reasons. The other important finding was that educated people as represented by university students, opposed the continuation of this custom for various reasons, mainly because it denied sexual fulfilment to women and for general humanitarian reasons. I had the impression that the community had become aware of its hazards and was looking for a change. My great opportunity came when I was chosen by the Faculty of Medicine of the University of Khartoum, to lead a research project on the subject of female circumcision in the Sudan. It fulfilled my ambitions to learn as much as possible about this custom, and to try to find a solution to the problem of its continuation. This book is based on material resulting from four years continuous work. It was in many ways a difficult and painful experience which nevertheless proved to be most rewarding.

No precise information was available about changes in the practice or attitudes among Sudanese, but there was a general impression that gradually, attitudes were changing. It was, therefore, considered that the time was ripe for a nationwide survey with the following objectives:

1) To determine the prevalence of the practice and types of female circumcision in the Sudan;
2) To identify the resulting health problems;
3) To outline the social, religious and traditional attitudes

towards the custom and hence to discuss possible ways
which could lead to its eradication.

It was planned that samples could be taken from all the six
former provinces of Northern Sudan, but because of the limited
time, and staff, only five provinces were included (see Map). The
Northern Province, which was the one to be omitted is inhabited
mainly by tribes which are distributed all over the Sudan, so that
they were, in fact, represented. The Southern region was excluded
because circumcision is not generally practiced there.

The sample — from both urban and rural areas — consisted of
3,210 women and 1,545 men. Separate questionnaires were used
for collecting the data. The one for women covered all aspects of
circumcision, attitude and personal data, while that for men
covered personal data and attitudes. Direct interviews were
conducted by persons of both sexes in visits to people's homes.

I collected additional data by visiting hospitals to enquire about
any complicated cases; where these were presented I interviewed
the victims. I also interviewed almost all the trained and untrained
midwives in the areas visited and contacted other health personnel,
such as principals of midwifery schools, assistant commissioners
of health, etc, to obtain information about the situations in their
areas.

This short study is based on the results of the survey, which was
the first to be carried out on this subject in the Sudan, and on
my M.Sc. thesis presented to the University of Khartoum in 1981.

Asma El Dareer

Areas Studied

1. Circumcision of Women and Factors Influencing the Practice

Circumcision is practised all over the studied areas (see Map)
with a prevalence of almost 99%, and with different ceremonies
varying from region to region and from tribe to tribe. Out of a
total sample of 3,210 women 3,171 (98%) were circumcised
and only 39 (1.2%) were uncircumcised. Out of these 2,636
(83.13%) were pharaonically circumcised, 386 (12.17%) had
had the intermediate type and only 80 (2.5%) had had sunna.
The remaining 69 could not be classifed because they said they
did not know which type they had undergone.

Factors affecting the practice, which will be described and
discussed in this chapter, are numerous, including types, age,
urban/rural distribution, religion, education and tribal.

The Three Types of Operation

Pharaonic: Infibulation
This is the oldest and most prevalent type, accounting for more
than 80% of the cases surveyed. There are two methods of
infibulation: the classical and the modernized. The former consists
of removal of the clitoris, labia minora and labia majora with the
two sides of the wound being brought together by different
methods. In Eastern Sudan adhesive substances such as sugar, egg,
cigarette papers are placed on the wound and left for three to
fifteen days; when it is discarded the dead tissue is taken away
with it leaving a small opening. In Central and Northern Sudan,
thorns with a piece of palm reed wrapped around are used. Sometimes a V-shaped splint, called a *gundura*, made from a bent piece

1

of palm reed is used, the free ends of the splint, being tied together. In Western Sudan sometimes adhesive substances, sometimes thorns, and sometimes strings are used. The girls legs are bound together in three places — at the ankle; above the knees; and round the thighs — for a period varying from 15 to 40 days, with the aim of limiting movement to allow proper healing. The main objective is to make the opening as tight as possible. Sometimes, to ensure tightness a thorn is inserted into the vagina so that when the tissue heals, only this opening will remain. Usually, to facilitate healing and prevent infection, warm oil, acacia tar, *merissa* (a local alcoholic drink) dough, or, in Western Sudan, animal excreta is placed on the wound. This classical type of circumcision is practised mainly in rural areas, but occasionally in urban areas too, in Eastern Sudan for example, where it is usually performed by untrained midwives, without anaesthesia. The time taken for healing varies between 15 and 40 days.

The modern type consists of removal of clitoris, labia minora and most of the anterior parts of the labia majora; the two sides are then brought together by stitching with catgut or silk. This is done by trained midwives, with anaesthesia in most cases, and usually in urban areas. Sometimes the legs are bound together as in the classical operation for up to seven days only. Warm oil, or warm tea or water are usually poured in the wound. Healing time varies between seven to fifteen days.

A more severe form is practised by the Shanabla tribe from Kordufan. In this type an additional V-shaped cut is made downwards of the vaginal orifice and the sides stitched together from below upwards to result in a very small hole. The girl who is circumcised in this manner is called *makhtoma*. The reason given for this particular practice is to protect the girl while she is out with the flocks of sheep as both females and males participate in looking after livestock.

Sunna

The Sunna is the mildest type, so called because it is thought to be the type recommended by Islam. The word 'sunna' means following the tradition of the Prophet Mohammed (blessings be upon Him). It consists of removing only the tip of the prepuce of the clitoris, and is, therefore, analogous to male circumcision. In some tribes this is accomplished by applying a heated piece of stone or pearl to the prepuce of the clitoris, i.e. burning it away. Sunna is the least common form of circumcision and accounted for only 2.5% of the sample surveyed. Both trained and untrained midwives perform this type of operation.

Intermediate

The intermediate type has varying degrees between sunna and pharaonic, and was invented after legislation forbidding pharaonic circumcision was passed in 1946. The British Government recommended the sunna type instead, which is why it is sometimes called 'Government sunna'. But the Sudanese found it difficult to change suddenly from pharaonic to sunna, which is considered to be no circumcision at all, thus this 'intermediate' type was invented by trained midwives as a compromise. According to Shandall (1967) it was invented by an Egyptian midwife called Hilbis, while Mcdonald (1948) attributed it to Miss Wolf, the principal of the midwifery schools. Under her guidance midwives were trained to do this modified form, which is why it is called

Stages of intermediate circumcision

In these 4 pictures, we notice how the child's face has been covered so that she cannot see the operation. She was also held down by a number of her relatives. Note the henna on her feet and hands, and the girtig.

1   2

1   *After administering anaesthesia, the trained midwife is cutting the clitoris, labia minora, and parts of the labia majora with scissors.*

2   *Stitching the wound with catgut*

3

3   4

3 *Application of penicillin powder*
4 *Putting cotton pads over the wound*

tahur El Dayat or 'midwives circumcision'; it is said to be replacing pharaonic. This operation entails removal of the clitoris, anterior parts or whole of labia minora, and slices, or more, of labia majora. The two sides are then stitched together leaving a variable opening which is sometimes the same as that of pharaonic, i.e., this intermediate type has different grades. The mildest form, which is wrongly considered as 'sunna', also has two grades or names. In one the clitoris is removed and the surface of the labia minora roughened to allow stitching. This is known as *sunna magatia*, i.e. 'covered sunna'. In the other, only the tip of clitoris or half of it is removed, the labia minora are intact and there is no stitching. This is known as *sunna kashfa*, i.e. 'uncovered sunna'. The most exteme form is that in which there is removal of the clitoris, the whole of labia minora, slices of labia majora, and stitching, more or less like the pharaonic. These different grades have arisen because the midwife follows the instruction of the girl's relatives who stand around telling the midwife to take this and leave that.

I attended circumcisions one day with a health visitor and saw four different grades. When the operator was told that the sunna type was required she did the mildest form. Midwives do not know what is meant by 'sunna' and consider the intermediate type to be sunna. They described the intermediate as when: 'a girl circumcised in this manner does not appear to be circumcised while standing, but it is clear when she sits', i.e. the labia majora are present.

The intermediate type is carried out in urban areas and in provincial capitals. Its incidence in the survey was about 12%, the highest incidence of intermediate after Khartoum (20.7%) being found in Gezira (16.9%), which may be due to the fact that Gezira is near to Khartoum. Some cases were brought from Gezira and El Obied to be circumcised in Khartoum because people think that circumcision in Khartoum is better.

In the intermediate type the legs are sometimes bound together but mainly at night to guard against movement during sleeping. It takes one to two weeks to heal.

Many differences were encountered between these three types as can be seen from Tables 1.1a to 1.1d, and several points emerged.

Table 1.1a
Types of Circumcision by Urban/Rural Areas

Place of Circumcision	*Sunna*		*Pharaonic*		*Intermediate*	
	No.	*%*	*No.*	*%*	*No.*	*%*
Urban	37	37.25	1,178	44.7	310	80.3
Rural	39	48.75	1,452	55.1	76	19.7
Not known	4	5	6	0.2	—	—

Table 1.1b
Use of Anaesthesia

	No.	*%*	*No.*	*%*	*No.*	*%*
Anaesthesia used	25	31.25	634	24.1	307	79.5
Anaesthesia not used	53	66.25	1,999	75.8	72	18.7
Not known	2	2.5	3	0.1	7	1.8

Table 1.1c
Use of Antibiotics

	No.	*%*	*No.*	*%*	*No.*	*%*
Antibiotics used	29	36.25	549	20.8	211	54.7
Antibiotics not used	45	56.25	2,081	78.9	168	43.5
Not known	6	7.5	6	0.2	7	1.8

Table 1.1d
Instruments Used

	No.	%	No.	%	No.	%
Sharp stones	6	7.5	13	0.5	–	–
Knives	31	38.75	1,170	44.4	–	–
Razors	20	25	837	31.8	87	22.5
Scissors	18	22.5	460	17.5	242	62.7
Not known	5	6.6	156	5.9	57	14.8

Place of circumcision: Pharaonic circumcisions mainly took place in rural areas (55.1%), whereas intermediate circumcisions were concentrated in urban areas (80.3%). The incidence of the sunna seemed to be the same in urban and rural areas.

Use of Anaethesia: The greatest advantage of intermediate circumcision is that it is almost always performed under local anaesthesia; this was used in around 31.15% of all circumcisions and in 79.5% of cases the intermediate of type, and 31.25% of cases of the sunna type. At the time of legislation (1946), the medical profession was against the use of anaesthesia in sunna circumcision for several reasons. It was said that the pain is practically negligible in the proper sunna; that the pain experienced in male circumcision was 1,000 times more severe and that in incision of tribal cheek cuts at least 10,000 times more severe. The operation would be quicker if no anaesthesia was used and that the administration of an effective local anaesthesia would cause as much pain as circumcision. It was also feared that injections carried out by untrained operators might be dangerous, causing sepsis or tetanus. Nowadays, however, sunna is always performed under local anaesthetic when it is done by trained midwives.

Antibiotics: Here, also, usually the intermediate form is systematically carried out with the protection of antibiotics. In 25.9% of all circumcised cases, and 54.7% of intermediate circumcisions antibiotics were employed. Local antibiotics, such as penicillin powder, were sometimes used. Antiobiotics served as a prophylactic measure at times, as well as for treatment. They are mainly administered by the trained midwives.

Instruments: The main instrument used for circumcision was a knife (38.5%), followed by razors (30.2%), then scissors (22.8%). Stones were rarely used (0.6%). When distributed by types, knives were the main instruments in pharaonic (44.4%) and in sunna

Instruments used for circumcision

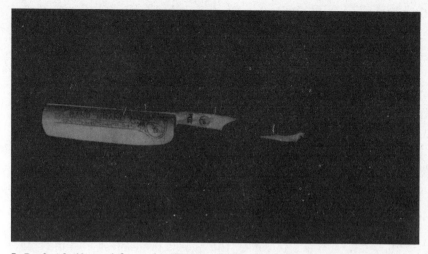

5 *Pocket knife, mainly used in Western Sudan for pharaonic circumcision*

6 *A locally made steel knife, with a wooden handle. Called* moos al arab, *it is mainly used in Eastern Sudan for pharaonic circumcision*

7

(38.75%) while for the intermediate, scissors were most commonly used (62.7%).

There are many types of knives: *moos al arab* locally made of iron with a wooden handle, used mainly in Eastern Sudan; a more specialized one *moos al shurafa*, used in the White Nile area; and an imported shaving blade, a sort of pocket knife called *moos afrengia*.

The problem is that these knives are not sterilized, but simply wrapped in a piece of old rag after use, without washing. Sometimes they may be wiped with oil and some midwives said that they heated it. But all the knives I saw were rusty, dirty and old. These knives were also used for deliveries and some midwives said that they used them in their housework.

The scissors, which were supposed to be part of a more sophisticated method, were not always sterilized, but were washed with water, with or without soap.

As for razor blades, usually one blade is used for one case, especially if it is brought by the people themselves. But in some cases it is also used more than once after washing only.

Sharp stones, as may be seen were used rarely, mainly in Eastern Sudan. Of course they are taken straight from the ground, with all the dirt on them. The cut with these stones is extremely painful, but apparently the victims could not feel it because they were so young at the time.

Excision

This type is not practised in Sudan but is included for the purpose of comparision. It is practised in some other African countries and consists of removal of the clitoris and labia minora but without stitching.

Extent of the Practice in Sudan

There are many different tribes in the Sudan (see Appendix III) which all have their own different customs. The practice of circumcision, being one of these customs, is subject to considerable variations. With very few exceptions all tribes in Northern Sudan practise some form of circumcision. These exceptions include the Fallata, Fur, Kinin, Nuba, all the four of which come from Western Sudan. Each has a reason for this. The Fallata people (who originate mainly from West Africa), are commonly divided into two main branches, Fallata Fota and Fallata Rattana. The

Fallata Fota (which means that they wear a small piece of cloth or scarf on their heads), do not practice circumcision at all. The Fallata Rattana (which means they speak a language other than Arabic) used to practise sunna type, but have changed to pharaonic as a result of their mixing with Arabs. It is a common belief among the Sudanese that only the Fallata do not circumcise women, which is why whenever anyone is asked why they do not abandon the custom, they will reply 'We are not Fallata' implying that anyone who is not circumcised must be Fallata.

The Fur tribe, who mainly live around Jabal Marra, Darfur province, traditionally do not circumcise their women, but those who came to the provincial capital of El Fashir or to nearby villages have begun to do so. The Medical Assistant in Tarni village (midway between Jabal Mara (Area of the Fur) and El Fashir) told me it was mainly inhabited by the Fur. I asked if circumcision was practised there, and if so which type and to what extent, because, although I had heard from the trained midwife that it was not, yet the interviewers found some women who were circumcised. He told me that it was not the custom of the Fur to circumcise women, but since they had come into contact with the urban areas, and due to the introduction of midwives, they had started to do so. That explains why I found that women of the younger generation were circumcised and the older ones were not.

A similar situation was found among the Nuba in Kordufan. The majority of the tribes who live around the hills do not practise circumcision, although some branches do perform clitoredectomy at certain times (according to Civsec Medical Records) some during the last weeks of pregnancy, and some at puberty. But those who come into contact with Arab tribes, such as the Talodi, and the Hawazma, or who came to live in the provincial capital of El Obied and central Sudan have started to circumcise women, even in the most drastic pharaonic form. They said that this was because they want to be like the Arabs. One Nubian lady said she was not circumcised till she came to live in El Obied, where she was circumcised after childbirth. She said she did this only because she had been constantly teased by her Arab neighbours; she also had her daughters circumcised.

Although the Southern region is not included in the sample, some southerners were interviewed because they happened to fall in the selected sample. Of these some mothers were not circumcised but their daughters were, having been affected by the values of their new society. Also some of them were circumcised after marriage, either at the request of their (northerner) husbands or on their own initiative. They stated that not all the southerners circumcise women, but that the practice is fairly widespread in Wau area. Wherever *Gallaba* or traders from the north are found, they said, there will be pharaonic circumcision. Certain unique traditions (Civsec Medical Records) are found among Southern tribes in which the womenfolk of tribal heads are pharaonically circumcised while the women of the tribesmen are circumcised by the sunna method. Alternatively, the tribal heads' women undergo sunna, while the tribesmens' women are not circumcised. Something similar is found among the Beni Helba tribe. The women of the *Nazir* (head of the tribe) were pharaonically circumcised whereas the rest of the tribe practised the sunna.

This distinction between types of circumcision for the female relatives of tribal heads and those of other tribesmen, emphasizes the importance of circumcision and the special status it confers.

The only tribe to remain unaffected is that of the Kinin from Darfur who live about a 1½ hour journey from El Fashir. It is claimed that they are not pure Sudanese, as they come from Chad. As Muslims, they believe that circumcision of any kind is against the teaching of Islam, which is why they do not practice it. As a consequence they face much contempt and ridicule from their neighbours. They have suffered from this situation because they are a small tribe and the people of the surrounding villages will not have any relations with them. This was clear from the way other people spoke about them when interviewed. Almost all of them said, laughing, 'If you want uncircumcised people, you can go to the Kinin village'. When asked why they spoke of the Kinin in this way they replied, 'We do not even visit them, because they are not circumcised.' Another problem faced by the Kinin was that trained midwives refused to stay with them because since they do not circumcise their women the midwife will not have this additional source of income. Kinin women thus have to depend upon untrained midwives and in complicated cases they must go to the midwives of the nearby villages. The Kinin, even their shiekh, are convinced that circumcision is not recommended by Islam, and too, they were aware of its hazards. Knowing that other Muslims did it, however, they wanted to be certain that they were right; they even asked me if I had read or heard anything about female circumcision in the Koran. Of course, I assured them that they were acting rightly.

These findings show that those tribes which do not practice circumcision at all are mainly from the Western Sudan. Nevertheless, the Zaghawa and Shanabla tribes, also from the West do perform the most severe form of pharaonic circumcision, using knives, without anaethesia or stitching. The Zaghawa were taken as an example whenever circumcision was mentioned. The term *Zaghawa circumcision* is used for a very severe form, where all the external genitalia is completely excised. One midwife described how she performed the operation:

> I hold the external genitalia from the junction of the two labia in my left hand, and the knife in my right hand. I cut the tissue from its roots and continue downwards, then I pass my hand over it. If I find any more tissue I will excise it totally. Next I put dough from merissa [an alcoholic drink locally fermented] or animal excreta on the wound, and press it very hard until the bleeding stops. Then the legs are bound together as usual. Healing may take up to 15 days, resulting in a clear, clean area. You can feel a skin over that area, without any flesh. This is why it is called *Tahara dalokia* i.e. just like a drum.

The Shanabla from Kordufan, perform their own type of circumcision, which is called *khitam* or *makhtoma*, as described earlier. So the two extremes were found in Western Sudan.

Other tribes who practice the pharaonic type only were those of Eastern Sudan: the Beja and Beni Amir. The intermediate type is not performed even in the urban areas; they do not consider sunna or intermediate to be circumcision at all.

The two main tribes to practise the sunna type, are the Rashayda from Eastern Sudan and the Messirriya from Western Sudan. Both are considered to be the descendants of Arab tribes, but the Rashayda are thought to come from El Hijaz. They said that they practised the sunna 'because it is sunna' or according to the practice of the Prophet. Also, being nomadic they said that they could not always find a midwife for a woman in labour, and women with sunna circumcision do not need much help when in labour, and she can usually deliver herself. Obviously they knew that pharaonic circumcision causes complications in childbirth. The Messirriya tribe also practiced the sunna both from the Islamic point of view and because it is their tradition. While the Rashayda continue to practice the sunna, the Messirriya began to

11

change to the pharaonic type, having been influenced by the surrounding society. We thus found mothers who were sunna circumcised while their daughters were circumcised pharaonically. I met such a woman in Omdurman and asked her why she was sunna and her daughter pharaonically circumcised. She said she had been circumcised in her village in Western Sudan, where sunna is prevalent, but her daughter was circumcised in Khartoum and that people around her there were pharaonically circumcised. The 'non-pure' Sudanese, Mawalid and Hadarma, mainly found in Eastern Sudan and the Khartoum area practice sunna circumcision.

The other tribes of Northern and Central Sudan, practice all forms depending on the situation. In the rural areas it is usually pharaonic while in the urban areas they have started to change to the intermediate type. Educated and religious families practice the sunna type, although they are a small minority.

The Berti tribe in White Nile area perform only the intermediate type. They do this, because as an Ansar sect, they follow the teachings of their political and religious leader, El Sayed Abdel Rahman El Mahadi.

Thus, generally, Eastern and Western tribes adhere to one form of circumcision, while the Central and Northern tribes are influenced to a large extent by contact with society.

Age at Circumcision

From Table 1.2 it will be seen that the most common age for under-going circumcision is six to eight years, with a maximum age of eleven years (2.6%); 18.1% of the girls were under five years of age at circumcision, including those aged from seven days to four years. The minimum age — seven to forty days — as we have noted, is found only among Eastern tribes, such as the Beja and Beni Amir. The reason for this is that so young a girl will feel nothing and the wound will heal quickly, in fact she will be healed at the same time as her mother. Whenever one sees a recently delivered woman with a baby girl most probably the child has been circumcised. I found this practice to be quite common in the Red Sea province in both urban and rural areas. In such cases classical pharaonic circumcision without stitching is performed, and occasionally the child's legs are bound together but for three days only, as by that time the wound will be healed. Oil is poured on the wound day and night to prevent infection. Circumcision of baby girls is, as might be expected,

Table 1.2
Age at Circumcision for Different Types

Age (in years)	Sunna	Pharaonic	Intermediate	Type not known	Total No.	%
Less than 5	10	503	48	13	574	18.1
Five	11	152	26	8	197	6.2
Six	9	404	58	5	476	15.0
Seven	20	450	74	11	555	17.5
Eight	12	350	64	15	441	13.9
Nine	8	275	42	14	339	10.7
Ten	10	327	37	3	377	11.9
Eleven	–	76	5	–	81	2.6
Do not know	–	99	32	–	131	4.1

performed for each child alone, contrary to the practice in those tribes where the age of circumcision is up to 11 years; here sisters' and brothers are usually circumcised together, and sometimes cousins too if they live near by or live in an extended family group.

But we found that girls were now being circumcised at three to five years of age. It was thought that the younger the better, and parents wanted their daughters circumcised before starting school at seven years old. Starting in the Khartoum area the practice of earlier circumcision is spreading to other areas. In some areas we also found girls circumcised at the age of two years, because it is believed to cure a childhood disease, known as *El Duda*, (the worm) or *El Kabrana*. A common practice in Western Sudan, it is found at times in other areas also. Sometimes relatives may notice that a girl is not gaining weight or is always ill or ailing; they then advise her mother to have her circumcised, believing that this will cure the child.

One of the midwives interviewed, in describing the worm disease said that its main characteristic is a sticky discharge causing the vulva to stick together. Even if there is no discharge the disease can be detected because the vulva will be thin and the clitoris very small, becoming even smaller even though the girl gets older. Burning micturition, rarely, urine retention and itching are symptoms of this disease. Its cause is unknown but thought sometimes to have been contracted due to the child having played by crawling or sitting on the ground when very young. But some girls are thought to be born with it.

13

The midwife said that she will know that this is the worm
disease at the time of circumcision, because a white worm will
jump out when she holds and cuts the clitoris and vulva; sometimes there are two or three worms. The blood of these children
will be very dark and sticky, like tar, and there will be only a
small amount. She firmly believed that by releasing the worm that
circumcision cures the complaint. I have been told of many cases
of this disease being cured by circumcision. In El Obied Hospital
I found a two year old girl who had been admitted for decircumcision due to urine retention after circumcision. Her grandmother
said they had her circumcised because she had the 'worm' disease.

Another curious explanation given for circumcising girls with
such a disease was that, if left uncircumcised they would become
prostitutes. No reason was offered for this belief.

From the foregoing it is clear that changes in the practice of
circumcision are not due to one, but to many factors in society,
including tribal traditions, urbanization, education, religion,
legislation and the introduction of trained midwives. The effect of
these various factors can be detected when comparing the type of
circumcision of female respondents with that of other members of
the family; mothers, sisters and daughters, as shown in Table 1.3.

It is interesting to note that the highest incidence of pharaonic
circumcision occurs among the mothers of respondents, decreasing
gradually with the elder sisters, respondents themselves, then
younger sisters, and sharply decreasing among daughters. The
opposite is true for the intermediate type. For sunna and no
circumcision the incidence is more or less the same. Also if we
look at the circumcision of daughters, we see little difference
between the pharaonic and the intermediate types, i.e. percentage-
wise they are approaching each other, but as usual pharaonic is
leading. Another important finding is that some respondents
quoted their daughters (i.e. group of sisters) as having been circumcised with a variety of types, e.g. one pharaonic, others intermediate or sunna. This also demonstrates that attitudes change
according to what is perceived as the norm in society.

Operators: Midwives and Others

About 92.5% of the total circumcisions (i.e. almost all cases) were
performed by midwives; in 58.4% of these cases the midwives were
untrained. Although sometimes to be found in urban areas such as

Table 1.3.
Type of Circumcision: Respondents/Other Women in Family

Type of circumcision	Mother	Elder sister	Respon-dent	Younger sister	Daughters
Not circumcised	1.2	1.1	1.2	1.4	0.9
Sunna	1.6	1.6	2.5	2.5	2.9
Intermediate	2.9	8.8	12.0	16.6	42.1
Pharaonic	92.7	87.2	82.15	77.1	50.1
Type not known	1.2	1.3	2.2	2.4	0.9
All types					3.2
Total Number	*3,210*	*2,526*	*3,210*	*2,442*	*2,630*

NB Results are taken as percentage from total number of cases in each
    column.

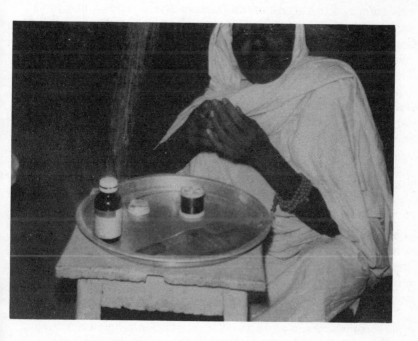

7 *An untrained midwife from Western Sudan with her instruments — the
   knife, thread, needles, and antiseptic. Some of these instruments are
   modern ones she has learned to use. She has also learned how to
   stitch and administer anaesthesia, i.e. just like the trained ones.*

El Fashir, El Obied, Sennar and Port Sudan, untrained midwives are mainly in rural areas. In the towns surveyed they are few and did their best to hide themselves, since they mainly perform the pharaonic types — with knives and sometimes scissors, but usually without anaesthesia or antibiotics. One midwife from El Kariba village near Medani, the capital of Gezira province, and another near Sennar, capital of Blue Nile province for example, had learnt the use of anaesthesia and antibiotics and regularly employ them.

A typical circumcision I saw carried out by an untrained midwife was as follows. A hole in the ground was covered by a mat with an equivalent hole in the middle. The child was brought by her relatives who held her down by arms and legs; and one of them hid her face with a piece of cloth; the midwife sat facing the little girl. Without washing her hands she took a knife in her right hand and held all the external genitalia in the left and cut off the tissue while the girl was struggling and crying. The relatives ululated, (shout *zagarid*) to drown the child's cries telling her that there was nothing to be afraid of, and that it would soon be over, and calling out the names of girls who had been brave. The poor child stopped crying either because she was tired or because her relatives put their hands over her mouth to prevent crying. After she had taken all the tissue, the midwife put either acacia, iodine, or salt or some other local materials on the wound and pressed hard. The limbs were then bound in three places and she was carried to the bed — where she may stay for up to 40 days — by one of her relatives.

Trained midwives are concentrated in urban areas and had performed about 34.1% of the circumcisions in the sample. They mainly perform the intermediate type, (about 90.4% of all cases of this type) using anaesthesia and antibiotics. They prefer not to do the sunna type, and even if they are asked for it, will do only the mildest form of the intermediate. The operation by trained midwives takes place on a table or bed, with a mat over it, where the girl is held down. The midwife may wash her hands with soap and/or water or antiseptic, or not at all. The genital area likewise may, or may not be washed, with or without antiseptic. In one case the nurse only wiped the area with cotton soaked in water; this nurse was the most dirty of them all. Some operators circumcise on an old, local bed without a mat, simply putting a dirty, old rag beneath the girl.

In all the cases I attended one needle was used for injecting anaesthesia, (without sterilization) and one needle for stitching.

The sister-midwife, and the health visitor poured antibiotic powder over the wound and covered it with cotton pads. There was no binding of the lower limbs.

In some rural areas where there are both untrained and trained midwives the bulk of the work is done by the untrained. It is not unusual to find them performing circumcision and deliveries whilst the trained midwife has no work. The untrained midwife is often preferred in rural areas because she is well known to the inhabitants — she is one of them. For this reason the newly trained midwives are chosen to serve in their home areas. Rural peoples also think that the untrained midwife performs her work better. Additionally, the trained midwife usually asks for a specific amount of money, especially for circumcision, while the untrained one accepts whatever is given her, sometimes even doing it without charge. I met one trained midwife in a village not far from El Obied who refused to do circumcision, since the people there were very poor and could not afford to pay the sum she charged (about two pounds). She pointed out that she does circumcisions to earn money, so why should she spend time for nothing? She also believed the superstition, that 'seeing a lot of blood results in blindness' so that was an added risk. I commented that she performed deliveries where there is also much blood, but she explained that this was her duty and therefore she must do it. (I think she said this because she was embarrassed to have shown that she was interested only in money). As a result of her attitude the people in that village had no choice but to take their girls to the untrained midwife, or to the trained midwife in a nearby village. A midwife from a nearby village also came, at a specific time of year to circumcise groups of girls.

The third category which constitutes 2.8% of the total number of operators is that of old women, and sometimes old men, who had inherited this job from their parents. Found in rural areas, they perform either the sunna or pharaonic types, with knives and without anaesthesia.

Doctors and nurses together constituted 2.2%, and doctors alone 1.6% of the total. Although they pretend that they do not perform pharaonic circumcision, according to the respondents 67.5% of all the circumcision performed by doctors are of the pharaonic type; doctors carry out the operation in urban areas and particularly in the capitals of the provinces. It is quite unacceptable for doctors to perform circumcisions. They excused themselves by saying that they operate in a hygienic way and have knowledge of the anatomy; that if they refuse it will be done by others. A similar excuse is given by the trained midwives. Doctors, like trained midwives, also use anaesthesia, antibiotics and stitching, and there is no binding of lower limbs.

Payment to the operator differs according to the area, the standard of living of the people, and the operators themselves. Untrained midwives usually get a maximum of £s.1.00 (£s = Sudanese pound) and sometimes also soap, tea and sugar. The fee for trained midwives in Khartoum and Gezira has now increased to £s.20, and for doctors between £s.20 and £s.50. In other areas the fee is £s.3 - 7. Some midwives ask for a definite sum of money, others accept whatever they are given. Considering the low salary of midwives, it is understandable that they consent to perform circumcisions. Some operators have left their government work and live solely on their earning from circumcision and recircumcision. During the season for circumcision, ('the summer holidays') an operator can perform up to 30 cases daily, and one health visitor in Khartoum performs up to 60 operations daily.

Having discovered that the midwives were the main operators, whenever I visited any area I asked about them, and in rural areas about the untrained ones in particular. Sometimes the presence of untrained midwives in a particular area was denied in the fear that I might report this to the authorities. In almost every village I found at least one untrained midwife and, with the assurance that I only wanted to talk to them, interviewed them. They were very co-operative and, with the exception of two, admitted that they did perform circumcision. (For some detailed interviews with midwives see Appendix V).

All the trained midwives said that they had not been taught how to circumcise, but only to decircumcise for deliveries. They were taught that sunna is preferable to pharaonic circumcision which is bad, but not instructed how to perform it, which is why almost all the midwives think that the intermediate type is sunna. The use of government instruments and drugs for circumcision is prohibited but midwives in fact do use them.

I met the principals of the midwifery schools in every area I visited; asking them about midwifery training; whether or not instruction on circumcision is included; and if they ever performed the operation. All of them said they did not themselves practice circumcision, neither did they teach the midwives how to perform this operation. On the contrary, they taught them that circumcision is harmful and they should not do it. All of them were very eloquent in explaining the hazards of circumcision, and although they were aware that the trained midwives in their areas did perform the operation said they were unable to prevent them. What they could and sometimes did do was confiscate their medical kits and thus prevent them from working, particularly if any serious complication arose.

They all said that they needed the co-operation of other medical personnel. I found an example of such co-operation in El Fashir area where the gynaecologist was very active in attacking the practice. He made it clear to the midwives that anyone who performed circumcision would be punished, by unconditional dismissal from midwifery practice. This was reflected in the fact that the majority of the people in Darfur area had become aware that circumcision is harmful and knew that midwives were forbidden to do it, and that the midwives who are known to perform circumcision denied it. I was told that one health visitor who had vehemently denied carrying out this operation had, in fact, the previous day circumcised two girls. Her denials demonstrated that she was afraid and also that efforts to prevent the performance of circumcision by trained medical personnel has some effect. She told me that she had been working for more than 15 years, and had learned how to circumcise from a famous midwife in Omdurman, who had one form of intermediate circumcision named after her. She went on to say that she stopped performing circumcisions when the gynaecologist in El Fashir forbade all the midwives to perform it. He had made it clear that any midwife found to be circumcising would never again be permitted to practice midwifery, which was why all the midwives in the province were afraid. Following this, she continued, all the families took their daughters secretly to traditional midwives in the nearby villages and had them circumcised there. There were many complications, which led the trained midwives to point out to the gynaecologist that people continued to have their daughters circumcised, and that it was preferable that it should be done hygienically and asked his permission for them to resume circumcising, but he refused it.

She told me that when she had performed circumcisions they were only the sunna type, which, to her, consisted of removing the head of the clitoris and stitching to prevent infection and contamination with dirt. She thought that the pharaonic circumcision was bad. She did not perform recircumcision, because it could lead to accumulation of blood, and other complications.

This created many problems for her, and the number of cases she delivered decreased because of it. Some women after she had delivered them, called in another midwife to recircumcise them. She reported such cases to the principal of midwifery in the area and the midwife concerned would be punished and consequently, the number of deliveries she performed further decreased. She had not had any complications due to circumcision to face, and saw only one case of decircumcision. A bride came to a health centre because she was so tight, and was referred to the hospital where she was working. The gynaecologist there took this as a typical case and collected all the midwives to instruct them in the hazards of circumcision. The young bride had been circumcised by a traditional midwife and had many deformities in the vaginal wall, and was found to be retaining urine and menstrual blood.

Tarni, a village midway between El Fashir and Jabal Marra, about three hours by car to the south of El Fashir, is inhabited mainly by the Fur, who as previously noted, used not to practice circumcision, but I was told by the Medical Assistant there that it is now a newly introduced custom. The trained midwife denied ever performing the operation and said neither did the three untrained midwives because it is not their custom. She said she did not know who did the circumcisions, she never asked, (although originally she had said it was not practiced in that area).

I asked her to accompany me to visit some houses. We came to a girls' school and stopped there. I began asking the little girls if they were circumcised. One said that she and her sister were circumcised together and another that she was going to be circumcised. When I asked them who the operator was they hesitated, looking at the midwife who I noticed signalling to them to say nothing. Then one girl said that the operator was a midwife but she did not know her name.

I then visited some women who admitted that their daughters were circumcised by a trained midwife, without giving her name. Another interviewer came in and told me that the operator is called 'M'. At this the midwife was obviously embarrassed and took me to the Medical Assistant. She had a talk with him, after which he explained that the midwife concealed her activities from me because circumcision is a new custom, and she knew that the government forbids it, in addition to the prohibition by the gynaecologist in El Fashir. Thus she was afraid, thinking that I was a government official checking who was doing the operation. Then she apologised to me. I forgave her and we became friends.

Other operators, on the contrary, denied nothing. They even agreed to have their interviews recorded, because they know that the officials are aware of what they are doing and even brought their own daughters for circumcision.

Socio-Cultural Influences

Religion

Of the women in the sample 98.2% were Muslim and only 1.2% were Christian; 98.4% of the men in the sample were Muslim. The Christian women were mainly Copts from the Khartoum area, and a few Nuba. As Table 1.4 shows, all Christian women respondents practiced pharaonic circumcision; none of them was uncircumcised or even had the sunna type. It might be claimed it is impossible to draw any conclusions from such a small sample but these were the only Christians who happened to be in the sample. Nevertheless this may go some way towards dispelling the idea that circumcision is solely an Islamic custom. Moreover, those women who did not practice circumcision were Muslims who said that to do so was against the teaching of Islam, as did the people of the Kinin tribe.

Table 1.4
Practice of Circumcision/Religious Affiliation

Religion	Not circumcised		Sunna		Pharaonic		Intermediate		Type not known		Total
	No.	%	No.	%	No.	%	No.	%	No.	%	
Muslim	39	1.2	80	2.5	2,578	80.31	386	12	69	2.15	3,152
Christian	–	–	–	–	58	1.81	–	–	–	–	58
Total	39	1.2	80	2.5	2,636	82.12	386	12	69	2.15	3,210

Yet it cannot be denied that a strong belief that circumcision is recommended by Islam does exist, especially among those who practice the sunna type; Table 1.4 reveals that only the Muslims practice the sunna type. There is also a Muslim sect called *Ansar El Sunna* i.e. 'supporters of sunna' found in the El Gadarif area in Eastern Sudan who insist on their womenfolk undergoing the sunna circumcision only. They are now holding a campaign for this movement. Yet what they are campaigning for is not the correct sunna, but what it is wrongly believed to be, i.e. the intermediate form.

Education

As a girl has no say in the type of circumcision she is to undergo it would have been pointless to seek the effect of education on the respondents themselves. To discover the effect of education we must examine the education of the parents as it is they who take the decision about circumcision. The majority (84%) of mothers, and 42.3% of fathers were illiterate. Tables 1.5a and 1.5b show that 31.3% of sunna circumcised respondents were daughters of *Khalwa* or Koranic school educated fathers. The educated mothers chose the intermediate type for their daughters.

Statistical evidence proved that a strong relationship exists between the type of circumcision chosen and parents' education. Daughters of highly educated parents are commonly either not circumcised at all, or if circumcised, the sunna or the intermediate type is chosen in preference to the pharaonic. The effect of religious education is demonstrated by the fact that the most common circumcision chosen by *khalwa*-educated fathers was the sunna type.

Although the number of parents who are highly educated is small, the effect is obvious.

Table 1.5a
Types of Circumcision/Education of Respondents' Fathers

Education	Sunna	Pharaonic	Inter-mediate	Type not known	Not circum-cised
Illiterate	12	1,170	117	54	5
Khalwa	25	788	118	–	13
Elementary	9	365	56	7	9
Intermediate	15	168	45	3	7
Secondary	12	75	12	–	–
Post-secondary	6	54	15	–	5
Not known	1	16	23	5	–

Table 1.5b
Types of Circumcision/Education of Respondents' Mothers

Education	Sunna	Pharaonic	Inter-mediate	Type not known	Not circum-cised
Illiterate	55	2,310	284	37	11
Khalwa	12	63	12	–	–
Elementary	6	167	18	–	4
Intermediate	6	36	33	–	5
Secondary	1	4	6	5	6
Post secondary	–	–	3	–	–
Not known	–	56	5	27	13

Urban/Rural Residence

1,610 (50.16%) of women respondents lived in urban areas and 1,600 (49.84%) in rural areas. As seen in Table 1.6 there is no difference in the overall numerical magnitude of the practice of circumcision between urban and rural areas, the same percentages were found in both. The main difference again lies in the types chosen. As a general rule the pharaonic type predominates in both areas. It has been proved statistically that there is a relation between urban/rural distribution and types of circumcision performed. This relationship is mainly seen when comparing the pharaonic and intermediate types. The incidence of the intermediate type in urban areas is almost double that in rural areas (67.9%), which suggests that the intermediate is replacing the pharaonic type in urban areas. This may be due to the fact that there are more trained midwives in urban areas, and also be related to the fact that people in urban areas are aware of the law prohibiting pharaonic circumcision. The incidence of sunna is more or less the same in both areas.

Urbanization also has the effect of introducing circumcision to communities which have never practiced it before. For example, the Fur tribe, who do not usually practice circumcision at all, started to do so when they migrated into the vicinity of urban areas; the Nuba were similarly affected.

Celebration Ceremony

The girl to be circumcised is called the 'young bride', because she is dressed like a bride, with new clothes, gold jewellery and is adorned with henna. She will either be circumcised at her home

Table 1.6
Types of Circumcision/Residence

Residence	Sunna No.	%	Pharaonic No.	%	Intermediate No.	%	Not known No.	%
Urban	42	1.32	1,257	39.64	262	8.26	34	1.07
Rural	38	1.20	1,379	43.49	124	3.91	35	1.1
Total	*80*	*2.52*	*2,626*	*83.13*	*386*	*12.17*	*69*	*2.17*

The figures are derived from the total number of circumcised respondents
(3,171) of whom 1,595 were urban dwellers and 1,576 rural dwellers.

or taken to the operator's house. In the past, circumcision always
took place in the early morning but now it is often done in the
evening. The women encourage the girl with *Zagarid*[1] and by
repeatedly saying she is brave and there is nothing to fear.

After the operation the child is laid on a bed and, *girtig*[2] is done
— although this is sometimes done before the operation takes
place. It is the custom of some tribes to take the girl to the river,
preferably at sunset.

8 *Black necklace, with red beads, used for* girtig, *to guard against the
evil eye, bleeding and infection*

The celebration which accompanies the operation follows a similar pattern for all social classes. Relatives are invited to meals, either on the day of the operation or the day preceding it — the 'henna day'. If only girls are to be circumcised then the guests are women only, but if boys and girls are to be circumcised on the same day then the guests are of both sexes. The celebrations may continue for three days.

The girls are given presents of money, gold and clothing by the guests; doubtless this contributes to a ready acceptance of circumcision and possibly explains why almost all girls questioned said that they had wanted to be circumcised and, although they were afraid of the operation itself, had enjoyed receiving the gifts. Uncircumcised friends of girls who have been circumcised happily anticipate their turn, when they too will receive many gifts. It is customary for girls to gather in a group and hold out a pot asking for money. All the guests at the celebration must contribute; the girls then either share it equally amongst themselves or buy fruits or sweets.

If a death has recently occurred in the family the celebrations will be postponed, but *girtig* and the visit to the river always take place, because these serve specific purposes. *Girtig* is to protect the girl from the evil eye and prevent bleeding; going to the river is a form of *mushahra* (treatment) for the state of *kabsa* (ritual danger) which affects newly circumcised girls and newly delivered women. It is an insurance against such problems as infection, urine retention or bleeding.

Only amongst the tribes of the Eastern Sudan, where circumcision of girls takes place between the ages of seven and forty days, are such celebrations an exception.

Nowadays, the celebrations have become modernized. Invitation cards are sent to the guests, a singer or dancer entertains them. This suggests that the practice continues to flourish and remain acceptable.

Influence of Age on Type Performed

Whilst the incidence of the practice is more or less the same for different age groups, the type differs between age groups (see Table 1.7). The main distinction is between pharaonic and intermediate types. The pharaonic is the type most frequently practiced for all ages, but with the highest incidence among the over 64 years group; only two respondents in this group were uncircumcised. The incidence of the intermediate, as a replacement for

Table 1.7
Types of Circumcision/Age of Respondents

Age Group (years)	Sunna	Inter-mediate	Phara-onic	Type not known	Total	Not circum-cised
Under 15	3	10	19	31	63	1
15-24	29	198	1,021	6	1,254	17
25-34	23	123	787	3	936	5
35-44	20	55	463	21	559	6
45-54	3	—	219	8	230	4
55-64	2	—	78	—	80	4
Over 64	—	—	49	—	49	2

the pharaonic type, increases with lower age groups. The maximum age of those with intermediate circumcision is the 35-44 year group; this coincides with the introduction of legislation forbidding pharaonic circumcision.

Notes

1. Ululation for a joyous occasion.
2. The ritual decoration ceremony, in which the girl is adorned with red thread, pearl necklace and a scarab; believed to stop bleeding and speed up the healing process. Performed either immediately before or immediately after the operation.

2. Health Problems Consequent upon Circumcision

As a surgical operation circumcision can be expected to have complications. Since this operation is usually performed by untrained people, ignorant of anatomy and under unhygienic conditions without sterile instruments and employing different local substances, post-operational complications are even more likely. It is thus very important to examine the incidence, patterns, methods of treatment and factors affecting the incidence of complications.

It is, however, one of the most difficult aspects to investigate in spite of framing questions in various ways. We would say, 'There are some who have experienced urine retention, or bleeding, did you face such things?' or 'Have you had *kabsa*?' or 'Do you have difficulty in micturating?' the usual answer was 'Thanks to God, nothing happened.' 'We usually do not have such things.' or 'Our circumcision was very good.' or even 'We have not heard of such things.' This is either because people will not admit to having these complications or because they do not relate them to circumcision, such as for example urinary tract infections, pelvic infections and infertility; complaints they will admit to when enumerated one by one. Some complications, such as bleeding and infection are attributed to *kabsa* and not connected with circumcision, because the women do not believe that circumcision is harmful.

It is also very difficult to obtain definite data on complicated cases from the hospital records. If they are there they do not represent the real picture for several reasons. 1) Since it concerns a sensitive part of the body, women are reluctant to seek medical advice. Sometimes they prefer to suffer rather than to go to a male doctor. 2) The usual type of circumcision is the pharaonic; knowing it is illegal, women try to hide the complications, especially the immediate ones, fearing enquiries about the operator and why they performed the pharaonic type. People will never reveal the name of the operator; they would sacrifice the life of their daughter first, because it is thought to be shameful to be an informer and it is not accepted in society. 3) The health services are not within easy reach of rural and remote areas, so if complications do occur no place for treatment and reporting is available. 4) Complications will be reported only if they are very severe and prolonged.

So the data obtained from hospital records and reported cases was extremely limited, and consisted of very severe complications only. The fact that of the 790 immediate complications following circumcision found in the survey only 94 (11.9%) cases were shown to medical personnel illustrates this. It could also mean that complications were not serious and could be treated locally; yet some women were in real need of medical intervention but their relatives preferred not to report their cases.

Any complication should be taken seriously and registered and reported to authorities, but what happens is quite the opposite. Of those cases that needed medical intervention, 84.5% were unreported. This again shows the strength of community relationships and explains why legislation alone is not enough. Even among 15 reported cases, only two operators were prevented from working, clearly indicating that the law is not strong enough to deter the operators. If it was strictly applied, all those who performed pharaonic circumcision should be imprisoned or fined, not only those responsible for post-operational complications.

Tables 2.1a and 2.1b summarizing the results of the survey in respect of complications, and classification by many writers on the subject indicate two main categories: i) immediate complications instantly following the operation; and ii) after-effects; that is, delayed complications from which a woman may suffer throughout her life.

The results presented in the tables represent the complications from which the respondents themselves said they suffered. These victims may face more than one, which is why percentages were calculated from the total number of complications and not from individual cases. My attempts to obtain statistical data from hospitals were fruitless. However, in every area surveyed I managed to visit the hospital to discover if there were any complicated cases at that time. In every hospital I found at least two cases of either immediate or delayed complications.

Table 2.1a
Immediate Complications/Types of Circumcision

Type of circumcision	Bleeding	Shock	Swelling	Fever	Wound infection; failure to heal	Difficulty in passing urine	Urine retention	Total	No complication
Sunna	5	–	–	–	–	–	2	7	74
Pharaonic	127	31	43	117	138	158	75	689	2,006
Intermediate	36	–	8	16	13	14	17	94	295
Total	*168*	*31*	*51*	*113*	*151*	*172*	*84*	*790*	*2,375*

Table 2.1b
Delayed Complications/Types of Circumcision

Type of circumcision	Painful scar Keloid	Vulvar Abscess	Inclusion cyst	Recurrent urinary tract infection	Chronic pelvic infection	Difficulty in penetration intercourse	Pain during intercourse	Difficulty in passing menses	Total	No complaint
Sunna	–	–	–	7	5	–	–	–	12	69
Pharaonic	9	128	16	225	208	196	51	36	869	1,776
Intermediate	2	15	3	51	28	35	5	3	142	310
Not circum-cised	–	–	–	4	3	–	–	–	7	30
Total	*11*	*143*	*19*	*287*	*244*	*231*	*56*	*39*	*1,031*	*2,185*

Immediate Problems

From Table 2.1a it can be seen that there are potentially two sets
of complications: such as bleeding, shock, infection, or swelling;
and those specifically related to the site of the operation, which
are urinary problems. The total number of immediate compliccations was 790, about 24.96%. When related to types of circumcision we see that the occurence in the pharaonic is 25.6%; in the
intermediate 24.1%, and only 8.1% for sunna. Included in these
complications are:

Difficulty in passing urine
This is the most frequent and constituted 21.65% of total complications. Almost all circumcised girls experienced pain and burning
micturition due to the raw wound, but difficulty in passing urine as
such is due to the small opening, i.e. tight circumcision. For the
pharaonic type it constituted 22.8% of all its complications and
for the intermediate type 14.99%. This may mean that it is
generally present in the pharaonic type.

Girls who may suffer in this way usually complain that they can
pass only drops of urine, or that micturition is very painful, or
that they need to spend a long time trying to micturate and strong
muscle contractions to help discharge the urine. This complaint
may be manifested in the first days after circumcision, as seen
from the following case, or this condition may continue for some
time before the sufferer complains. Decircumcision is indicated
but this is rarely done and some cases are neglected until it is
almost impossible to pass urine.

A little girl, five years of age, from Sennar, had been pharaonically circumcised seven days before, by a trained midwife. When
her mother noticed that she could pass only little drops of urine
she was brought to hospital and decircumcised. Unfortunately the
wound became infected and she had a longer than normal stay
in hospital.

Urine retention
This condition is found in all three types of circumcision, and
can arise:
a) Reflexly, because of fear of passing urine in the raw area, which
is why it is present in all three types. Here the child starts to pass
drops of urine and then stops and refuses to continue, saying that

A complicated case of an infected circumcision wound

9 *Before hospitalization*

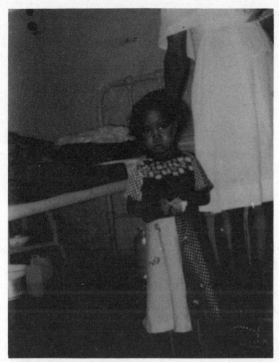

10 *And after*

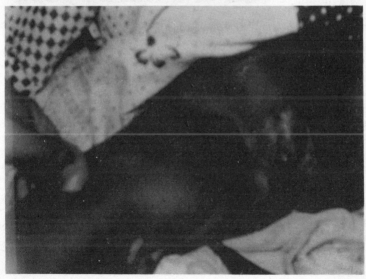

it hurts, or she is afraid it will be painful. She will cry whenever asked to pass urine. It is usual for girls to avoid urinating on the first day of circumcision; they will do so only when they feel unable to retain urine any longer.

b) Retention due to tight circumcison or completely obliterated orifice. These are cases which need immediate relief. Some may retain urine from the first day, and some later as a result of infection. It is usually relieved by decircumcision and is found only in the circumcision of the intermediate and pharaonic type.

A four year old child, pharaonically circumcised 15 days before, was brought to hospital complaining of urine retention. After examination the doctor told her relatives that she needed decircumcision and that he would do it. When the relatives, heard the term decircumcision, they presumably thought this would spoil her circumcision. Before preparations for the operation were completed, they escaped, taking the poor child with them. God knows what happened to her.

c) Injury to other parts. This is a rare complication, but does happen, especially in the pharaonic type. Here the urethra may be damaged, and it becomes worse when infection has followed. This is a predictable accident of trauma, due the following facts; the girl is small and frightened; the operator is unskilled; the nature of the operation itself, which consists of holding all the tissue (external genitalia) and cutting it away; no anaesthesia is used in most cases.

So the girl is struggling and the operator wants to finish as soon as possible. I was told of one case like this in El Fashir. The child, who had been pharaonically circumcised by an untrained midwfie, died as a result. Injuries must be treated by doctors; failure to ensure this caused this child's death.

Methods of treatment for urinary complications differ, according to the cause, the operator and the place of residence. Sometimes the relatives try to treat the problem by sitting the girl in hot water; this remedy is also used by some midwives. This was done in 177 cases. The relatives may frighten the girl, saying they will call the operator to circumcise her again if she does not urinate. This could be effective if the cause is simply fear of passing urine, but if there is really tight circumcision something more is needed. The usual procedure is to call the operator to treat the case. (Different methods are described in the discussion on decircumcision.)

Haemorrhage (Bleeding)
This is the second most common complication, accounting for
21.3% of the total number (790). It occurs in all three types of
circumcision and is common in the sunna type, which is why
the midwife sometimes stitches in this type. Haemorrhage can
either be primary, from injuries or arteries or veins, or secondary,
as a result of infection.

Bleeding can be very severe and sometimes fatal and ten of
those surveyed had suffered from shock and needed medical intervention. Slight bleeding is treated either by compression or by
applying salt. The primary reason for going to the river or *gertig*
is to obviate bleeding. In some cases, when bleeding develops the
girls were immediately taken to the river to wash their face in it
and drink some water.

In Omdurman Civil Hospital in 1977 I saw a girl of seven years
old who had been pharaonically circumcised 15 days before. Three
days after circumcision the wound became infected and began to
bleed. Because the child had been circumcised by a trained
midwife her relatives were hesitant about taking her to the
hospital. She was finally brought to hospital with severe anaemia;
her haemoglobin count was only 20%. She urgently needed, and
was given, a blood transfusion.

Infection
Infection is potentially inevitable in view of the unhygienic way
the operation is performed and the type of instruments used,
which vary from stones to knives and razors — generally not
sterilized. Scissors were sometimes sterilized but knives were
simply washed in water or oil, or wiped with a dirty, old rag. Other
sources of infection may be substances applied locally to the
wound such as goat excreta, mainly used in Western Sudan; this
can lead to tetanus. Infection in itself can result in failure to heal,
so the wound has to be restitched. The use of antibiotics whether
systemic or local may help to decrease its incidence. Infection is
also sometimes perceived as related to the evil eye.

I saw a case admitted to the gynaecology ward of Senner
Hospital. It concerned a four year old girl from Diem El Kabir, a
small village near Sennar. The child had been pharaonically
circumcised along with her two elder sisters 47 days before by a
trained midwife with the aid of anaesthesia, antibiotics, and
catgut sutures.

The child's mother said that the wound healed very well until

the 22nd day when the girl began to cry because of itching and
pain at the site of circumcision. Her mother found that there was
a swelling on the right side, and the girl was feverish. She took her
to the midwife, who gave her injections. The child improved but a
week later the same complaint recurred. Her mother discovered a
swelling on the left side this time. She took her for treatment to
the Medical Assistant. It happened that the mother was in hospital
with her younger child; upon being discharged she found her
daughter febrile and vomiting. She took her to the paediatric
clinic where the circumcision was found to be infected and there
was a gaping of the wound about two stitches long; there had been
no urinary complications. The wound was opened and cleaned in
the hospital.

The child's grandmother said that when they first noticed the
infection they had made a paste of ground 'senna senna' herbs and
water and put it on the wound but there was no improvement.
Then they obtained *higab* (an amulet) and *mihaia* and *bakhrat*[1]
(traditional cures) from their Sheikh, as the grandmother related
the infection to the evil eye.

Fever
This can be fatal; the cause is either infection or loss of blood. The
usual traditional treatment is going to the river, as it also is
believed to be related to the evil eye; another traditional method
of treatment is to massage the patient with oil.

Shock
From the results of the survey this occurs only in cases of pharaonic circumcision. There are two types of shock: neurogenic,
due to severe pain and fear; and haemorrhagic, due to severe
bleeding. Of the 31 shocked cases in the survey, 10 were haemorrhagic, and the remaining 21 were neurogenic. The pain of the
operation, especially when it is performed without anaesthesia, is
so severe as to lead to shock. To guard against fear, sometimes the
girls were taken to the *faki* before the operation, as described
later.

Arthritis
This is very rare and I was surprised to come across such a case.
Two girls 9 and 10 years of age from Omdurman were to be
circumcised; the family had asked me to attend as they wanted
them to have the sunna operation. I accordingly accompanied

them and asked the operator to perform only the sunna type. The relatives who accompanied us disagreed with this, but I assured them that it was the wish of their mother. The nurse did perform the sunna, but one hour later the children were taken back to the operator, who circumcised them again with the intermediate type. Five days later the elder sister developed fever, pain in the right leg and inability to walk. On examination she had swelling and tenderness at the right ankle joint. She was treated with heavy antibiotics and responded dramatically. Her sister, who had also been circumcised twice, did not develop any similar complication.

Long-term Problems

From Table 2.1b it can be seen that the occurrence of all delayed complications is 32.2%, i.e. 1,023 cases. For each type alone, the percentage for pharaonic is 32.85%, intermediate 31.4% and sunna 14.8%.

Delayed complications can also be divided into two categories: a) Local effects: i.e. at the site of circumcision, such as the results or effects of tight circumcision; vulvar abscess and inclusion cysts; effects on child-bearing. b) Systemic effects, which include urinary complications (urinary tract infection) and chronic pelvic infection. These are the most common and present in all types of circumcision. Although they are sometimes present in uncircumcised women, circumcision aggravates them.

Local effects

The results or effects of tight circumcision include difficult or impossible penetration and pain during intercourse, and difficulty in passing menstrual blood. These conditions constituted about 31.86% of complications. They are present only in the pharaonic and intermediate types.

Difficulty in penetration: This is the most common, and it may be a long time before the husband can effect penetration. The treatment for this — decircumcision — is discussed later in the section on circumcision and sex. Of the 231 respondents who had this problem, 66 needed decircumcision.

Pain during intercourse: This was reported by some 56 women (2.46%), and is usually due to tight circumcision and rigid fibrous tissues which have lost their elasticity; or it may be due to tears and injuries resulting from vigorous initial sexual acts. The results can be serious; it may lead to frigidity, and to psychological trauma or impotence in men. For women, difficulty in penetration and painful intercourse may cause them to hate sex and find no enjoyment in their sexual life. Two women preferred anal intercourse because of the pain of normal intercourse. Some admitted that they enjoyed or had normal sex only after delivery, because the tightness was relieved.

One 45 year old woman from El Obied whom we interviewed told us that she had been pharaonically circumcised and was married at the age of 15. She said, 'Our custom is to stay with our husbands only in the evening during early married life. My first sexual experience was very painful because I was so tight, and the following experience was equally painful. On one occasion my husband tried to force penetration and the flesh tore. This wound became infected, so sexual intercourse became even more painful for me. I wanted to spend the nights with my family, and hated to go to my husband, but my mother compelled me. I hated to have sexual relations, and my husband complained about this. I was so pleased when I became pregnant, because the tradition in our tribe is that a husband may not have sexual intercourse when his wife is pregnant. When I was delivered the opening became wider and I could have normal sexual relations. But my sex life is still of no enjoyment or interest to me, I perform it merely as a duty.'

Menstrual Complications: These may be present as pain during menstruation — a very common complaint amongst all Sudanese women, especially the unmarried ones. It is due either to the small opening or to chronic pelvic infection. Some respondents said that they were relieved after marriage or delivery, which proves that it is due to the small opening. It may also be present as difficulty in passing menstrual blood, i.e. passing a very small amount of blood and the menstrual period taking an abnormally long time; or failure to pass blood. This condition will be noticed at the time of menarche and usually the girls are too shy to complain and remain in this state until marriage, or sometimes the parents know enough to seek medical advice. The usual treatment is decircumcision.

One 18 year old girl from El Obied suffered discomfort and pain three days before the menstrual cycle started. When it did start the blood came in a small amount for the first two days, with fever and vomiting; on the third day the flow increased a great deal and continued for seven days. She was hospitalized several times and told by the doctor that her condition was due to circumcision and that she should be decircumcised, but she refused.

Sometimes the results of such a condition may be very serious. One poor girl lost her life because of this. She had such a tight circumcision she could barely pass any blood from her first menstrual cycle, her following cycles were the same. She was too shy to tell her mother about this, and the accumulated blood led to an increase in the size of her abdomen. This, together with the absence of menstrual blood made her family think that she was pregnant and she was killed to save the family honour.

Another girl, aged 15, whom I attended in Omdurman Civil Hospital in 1978, was brought in secretly by her mother who wept while explaining the complaint, and constantly asked us not to tell anyone about it. She said that she noticed that her daughter had reached puberty, but that she was not having her periods; she also noticed that there was a gradual increase in the size of the abdomen. She became worried and afraid and began to question her daughter suspiciously. The girl said she had never had periods, so her mother had brought her to find out whether or not she was pregnant. The girl was found to have a pinhole circumcision and her mother was assured that this was not pregnancy. The girl had been pharaonically circumcised and her mother said she had difficulty in passing urine. The girl was decircumcised, and to the astonishment of her mother a large amount of dark, offensive smelling blood was released.

Vulvar Abscess and Inclusion Cysts: These are present only in cases of intermediate and pharaonic circumcision, since they are related to stitching or the parts taken; they are common gynaecological complications. The inclusion cyst results from part of the skin becoming embedded inside during stitching, or damage to Barthloin's duct and hence accumulation of its fluid. The cyst will increase and may reach the size of an orange, and become infected at any stage. The problem is that women will be shy, even the married ones, to show it, and will say nothing until it is accidentally detected on medical examination, or sometimes during labour, or when it is infected they will seek medical help because of pain.

I have seen one women in Omdurman Civil Hospital with a large inclusion cyst, almost like an orange. She came only because her husband complained that this disturbed him during intercourse. She was treated by excision.

One young girl sought medical advice only when she was about to be married, although she had noticed the cyst growing in size. She attributed it to different things, and even thought she may be changing her sex, because it seemed as if it was growing into a penis. She was worried, but kept silent because of shyness.

Young or unmarried girls may for example, tell their mothers that they have a swelling, or their mothers may notice they are ill and can detect the condition. Some prefer to treat it by traditional medicine rather than show it to a male doctor. Vulvar abscess is found in every day practice in hospital gynaecological departments.

Obstetric Complications: These are present only in cases of pharaonic and intermediate circumcision, from which both the mother and the newborn infant suffer.

Women in labour face many difficulties due to circumcision. These include: problems attendant in the necessary vaginal examination of a woman in labour due to tight circumcision. (One woman in Port Sudan needed decircumcision for this.) Circumcision causes delay in the progress of labour, especially in the second stage. During contractions, when the baby is coming down, the fibrous vulvar tissue fails to dilate to allow normal passage. The woman will continue bearing down until she is exhausted, and the baby's head will continue to push into this fibrous tissue, and cannot emerge unless incisions are made to widen the opening. If this is not done the head in pushing hard against the scar tissue, may cause perineal tear and laceration. One midwife said that, she is so happy when she delivers an uncircumcised woman, noticing the smooth progress of labour. But in a circumcised case, she is tense and anxious as she watches the woman's suffering until she has been delivered.

In addition, the continuous pressure of the baby's head causes death of the tissue, leading to fistula (abnormal passage), either between the bladder and the vagina or the vagina and the rectum. It was found that circumcision, mainly the pharaonic type is the main predisposing factor in formation of fistulae. It is very common among Western Sudanese women, complicated by the fact their husbands usually left them because the fistula causes incontinence and an unpleasant smell. There are many such cases in Khartoum and El Fashir Hospitals. It is a very difficult condition to treat and women who suffer from it stay for long periods — even years — in hospital. To cure it needs a very delicate operation, which is not always successful.

Another complication, that may occur if the midwife is delayed, is rupturing of the uterus as the baby cannot find a way out.

It is necessary for all circumcised women to be cut when in labour, in order to widen the opening for delivery. Incisions, which may be along the circumcision scar or laterally to it, depending on the person attending the delivery, are liable to bleeding and infection. This is one of the main causes of puerperal pyrexia and septicaemia. The following experience of a 35 year old woman from Para, a town in Western Sudan, is typical of this condition.

There is a rural hospital in Para, but it lacks enough trained midwives. When I saw her, this lady had been delivered 15 days previously, attended by a traditional midwife. When I entered the house to interview her she was lying ill in bed, febrile and jaundiced. I apologized for my intrusion and explained why I had come. Her response was that circumcision was the cause of all her problems.

She went on to tell me that she had been pharaonically circumcised by a traditional midwife. When her labour pains started she could not find the trained midwife and had to call in an untrained one, who delivered her by using a rope (the traditional method of delivery in the Sudan is in a crouching position with the woman holding on to a rope) and a knife. The wound failed to heal, and the midwife neither treated it nor returned to wash or even visit the newly delivered woman.

'I noticed that the wound, which was not healing, had an unpleasantly smelling discharge' the woman told me. 'I am treating it myself with hot water. The knife the midwife used was prepared by my husband and after delivery was wrapped in an old rag.' She also said that she had three daughters, all of whom she had had pharaonically circumcised by a traditional midwife because 'her circumcisions are good'.

Circumcision creates many problems for Sudanese women who are delivered outside their country. Foreign midwives or doctors do not recognize the scar and think that it is some abnormality or disfigurement. With luck the woman can explain herself or find someone who can, so that she can have an anterior episiotomy. If not, she may be subjected to multiple incisions, or possibly a Caesarean section. Many Sudanese women have had section performed abroad only for this reason. If an anterior episiotomy is done it will not be stitched, but most women are stitched when they return to the Sudan. Usually Sudanese women abroad are delivered by Egyptian or Pakistani doctors because they are aware of the condition.

Effects on the New-born: Prolonged labour can lead to intra-uterine foetal death; obstructed labour can also lead to foetal loss, and brain damage, resulting in handicapped babies.

Anterior and anterior-lateral episiotomy is not always safe, especially when it is done in a hurry; the presenting part of the foetus may be injured. I saw a five month old infant in El Fashir, with a deep wound in his forehead, as a result of being cut with a knife. In all that time, the wound had not healed and was infected. Scars resulting from such cuts are quite common, especially for those whose mothers were delivered by untrained midwives.

Systemic Effects

Urinary Tract Infections: These accounted for 24.54% of cases in the survey. In the pharaonic and intermediate circumcision the external meatus is covered by a skin flap, so that the inner epithelial surface of this area cannot be washed, consequently it becomes irritated by residues of urine, and prone to bacterial infection which may result in urethal stricture. I have seen a woman in Khartoum Hospital who complained of itching and burning micturition for which she had received treatment several times but it still recurred. All the investigations were normal; then a cystoscopy was recommended. When this was about to take place a stricture was found which was related to circumcision. Cystoscopy, in fact, relieved this case because it effected dilation. The woman was treated with antibiotics and the condition was successfully cured.

Chronic Pelvic Infection: This condition, due either to the small opening and collection of discharge, or to previous infection at the time of circumcision leading to ascending infection, accounted for 23.8% of cases. It is the main cause of infertility due to obstruction of the Fallopian tubes. It is a common complaint among Sudanese women, but they do not connect it with circumcision. They usually say, 'We have infections', and by this they mean chronic pelvic infection.

Circumcision and Sexual Relations

As sex is considered a taboo subject in Sudanese society it was difficult at first to ask questions and discuss such matters. Such questions needed time to enable us to build up a relationship with the respondents and gain their confidence. Moreover sex is believed to be only for men since the women regard the money the men give their wives as payment for this; women thus do not feel they are in a position to discuss it. Nevertheless, the answers were frank and useful. Some women first laughed, and called upon their friends to hear what we were asking. They said that this was the first time they had been asked about so private a thing.

It has been postulated that circumcision has many effects in sex. This is reflected in the response to the first sexual intercourse, time taken for full penetration and the enjoyment of sex itself.

I found that the majority of married women (81%) had been fearful of their first sexual intercourse. 65.8% of these gave circumcision as the main reason for this fear. The women said 'Of course we were afraid. This was the first time for us'; 'Every bride will be afraid.' For men the opposite seemed to apply. Only 13.4% said they had been afraid, saying that 'A man should not be afraid' or 'Why should we feel fear?' The small percentage who admitted to feeling afraid gave the fact of circumcision as their main reason (79%).

It is not uncommon to find brides very upset and anxious during the first days of marriage. This is due to many factors not immediately obvious: the events of circumcision itself; the preparation of the girl for marriage; the horrifying tales she has heard from her friends about sexual intercourse; and in some tribes, the fact of relatives waiting outside the marriage room to see the piece of cloth spotted with blood proclaiming that the bride is a virgin. Especially in Western Sudan, this cloth is hung outside on top of the house or hut. It is called *tobe el sharaf* 'the dress of honour'. After this event, the bridegroom gives the bride money and clothes. The narrower the opening of her vagina the higher the value of the gift. This procedure indicates the importance of pharaonic circumcision in these communities. It is really an examination for both husband and wife. If the cloth is not displayed this means that something is wrong, and either the bride will be in trouble, or the bridegroom will be considered a failure. He will try his best to successfully penetrate his bride, especially since sometimes a man called a *wazir* (brideroom's friend) attends the act with him. If the bridegroom finds his bride to be good and tight, he will give her mother a cow or money. If he does not, which implies that she has had previous sexual experience, the outcome depends on the groom. Either he prefers to keep this secret and gives the cow or money to his mother-in-law anyway, or he refuses and everyone will know the truth. It is really very difficult for a man to declare himself a failure, so he may resort to other than natural means to effect penetration, as will be seen later in this section. But if he declares that his wife is too tight, then this will be a credit to the bride, and her family, especially if she needs to be decircumcised. In this case the bridegroom should give the bride more money, called *sharaf* price (honour price) which may be gold, one or two ounces, as he can afford. It will be delcared to the public saying that 'her husband admitted it'.

The customs and traditions governing this matter vary from tribe to tribe and even from village to village. I discovered a strange custom in one village in the Blue Nile area. Here, the bridegroom must have a friend with him on the first day; his task is to tie the bride to the bed, then the husband should open her with a razor, either upwards or downwards and attempt to have intercourse. After which he displays the blood spotted cloth and dances with it. This practise is potentially dangerous; there may be severe injuries or the cut may be made in the wrong direction.

In contrast, there is a tribe in Western Sudan in which the husband is not allowed to use any unnatural means, even if he completely fails to attain penetration. He is supposed to tell his *wazir* who, in turn, will tell the husband's father who then tells the bride's relatives of the situation. They will take her to the hospital for decircumcision because it is far away and so can be kept secret. If the midwife decircumcised the bride it would soon be common knowledge and this would disgrace the husband.

Respondents answers to the question of how much time elapses before penetration is achieved, revealed that this depends on the type of circumcision, and, interestingly, a disparity between the answers of men and women.

Sunna circumcision was said to need less than a week, similar to uncircumcised cases. One man said 'Sunna circumcision will not take me a minute', because there is no stitching. The pharaonic was said to take up to eight weeks normally, and the intermediate somewhere between.

Of women respondents 52.6% said the average time was between one and two weeks, and 23.5% said three to four weeks. The remainder gave times ranging from five to eight weeks. The majority (75%) of the men interviewed gave less than one week; 19.6% said one to two weeks, and 5.4% up to nine weeks. This disparity could mean either that the women were exaggerating or the men minimizing the time required; or possibly that the men wished to give the appearance of virility. Many of the men and women interviewed were husband and wife and a comparison of 48 couples reveals that the average time given by the wives was between one to two weeks, and by the husbands less than a week.

Tightness of circumcision, which may lead to difficulty in penetration leads some men to seek a means of assistance. 5.5% of both men and women admitted to using lubricants such as Vaseline; also some used lubricants and attempted to dilate the vaginal passage with their fingers.

Bridegrooms usually continued to try these safe methods; and, if they failed think of other means. Much depends on the understanding between the couples. The wiser ones knew that the best remedy was to consult a doctor or a midwife, or go secretly to the hospital. This was in fact done by 10 male and 53 female respondents. The usual solution is decircumcision. One man from Khartoum had consulted the doctor before pursuing penetration, because he found the opening was too tight; his wife was decircumcised. In El Fashir Hospital I met a woman whose husband had brought her for decircumcision after he had failed to have normal sexual relations with her. She was 20 years, and told me that she was *makhtoma* (i.e. has tight circumcision). She had been married for one month, and her husband's attempts at penetration had resulted in *hufta* (i.e. invaginated skin near the original vaginal orifice). She had been pharaonically circumcised at the age of nine years, and had experienced difficulties in urinating and passing menstrual blood, but had never complained; she almost always had dribblings of urine. She was decircumcised under general anaesthesia, the day after my visit to her.

Some men, because of their masculine pride used instruments such as scissors or knives, or even chemicals. All the male respondents denied this, but 13 women said that their husbands decircumcised them in this way. Three of these were interviewed together with their husbands, but the husbands denied having done this, maybe they were embarrassed or afraid they would be accused of uncivilized behaviour. Some midwives had such cases brought to them for treatment. One said she remembered a bride, whose husband cut her downwards almost reaching to the anus. She was taken to her crying. The midwife said she could treat her but her husband must not attempt to have intercourse with her for at least 40 days. When he agreed to this she stitched the wound from downwards and made a cut upwards.

In another case the husband had tried to open his bride with a razor and had made a big cut upwards, like that for delivery. The bride was in great pain and her husband went to the midwife screaming 'Help me. I have killed my wife.' She went to his house and found his bride crying 'I am ashamed; I am injured, I will have

A case of tight circumcision where the woman needed deinfibulation upon marriage (makhtoma)

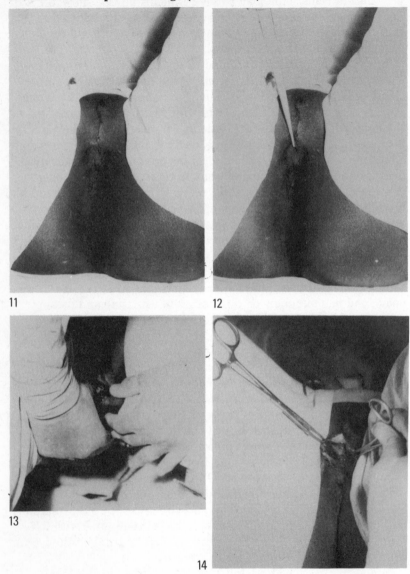

11 *Showing complete obliteration of the vaginal orifice*

12 *A forceps pointing to the pinhole opening of the vagina*

13 *Doctor probing for the opening during deinfibulation*

14 *Cutting or splitting of the circumcision scar during deinfibulation operation*

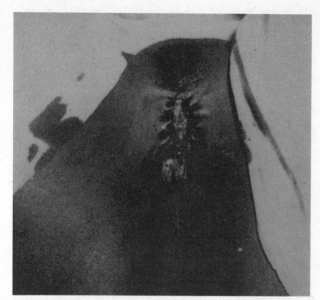

15 *The two cut sides now separately stitched leaving a fairly wide vaginal opening following completion of the deinfibulation operation*

a fistula.' Her relatives were all around her and the midwife told them to boil water and washed the wound thoroughly. Examination showed that there was nothing really wrong; there was no tear. Because of the pain she had jumped when her husband tried to cut and this resulted in a large wound. The bride's parents agreed that the midwife should treat her, but her cousins refused and reported the case to the police. The bride was taken first to the police station and then to the hospital where she told the doctor that her husband had smoked a green cigarette, insulted, and threatened to kill her, tied her up and cut her with a knife. Her uncle had told her to say this, she also told the same story to another midwife; saying that she had been sleeping when she felt something cutting her.

After this story the doctor had refused to treat her and she was kept in hospital for three days without treatment. Her husband was arrested, but was set free after investigations. Meantime, her relatives took her secretly from the hospital and the wound (by that time infected, but she recovered) was stitched by a midwife.

In court the judge had asked her whether she wanted her husband or her family; she chose her husband, but he and his father-in-law again quarreled and were both imprisoned. They commented that they are having all these troubles over 'a female sexual organ'.

Another midwife told how the friends of one man advised him to use acid (*moyat al nar*) because the opening would be tight. Then he followed their advice, and poured the acid on the bride's vulva, which affected all the area to the anus and she was crying. When her husband tried to effect penetration his penis was also affected and he jumped off, crying. They called the midwife, but did not say the injury was due to acid. The wound was stitched but did not heal until she was taken to the hospital. Her husband was so embarrassed that he went to a distant hospital for treatment.

This particular man's action became talked about by everyone in the hospital or outside. The men said 'Let him come to us and we will teach him a lesson. If he was not man enough himself, he should have brought her to us to open her for him'.

The father of another man who used acid threatened to kill him. After these cases people were forbidden to use acid. A man who uses any artificial means to effect penetration is not considered to be a real man.

Fearing the gossip and derision of the community some husbands prefer to take a longer time rather than use artificial aids or seek advice. One man said that he would prefer to die rather than ask for help, 'Do you want people to say that I am not a man?' This attitude is quite incredible since we found one woman who had remained tight for more than six years. This was discovered only when she came for treatment for infertility, for which the only cause was tight circumcision.

From the results of the survey, I found three pharaonically circumcised women who said that to achieve full penetration had taken 18 months. Five men said it had taken them from 6 to 18 months. Moreover, out of the total sample of 3,210 women and 1,545 men, seven women and five men had not experienced full penetration. The duration of their marriages varied between three months and two years. They said they could not ask for any help because they were ashamed of admitting to this problem.

Tears and bleeding usually follow the first sexual acts; these may be slight and are considered to be quite normal. These 728 women (31.9% of those interviewed) who had slight bleeding and tears considered this to be normal for every bride. The 59.1% who denied either tearing or bleeding commented, 'We have nothing abnormal'. 6.2% said that they had severe tears and bleeding, needing medical intervention. While two brides who had suffered similarly had not sought medical advice because they were ashamed.

The tears and bleeding indicate what may be a serious injury; sometimes due to the use of instruments or chemical substances by the husbands, as has been seen from the cases already described. Or it could arise normally when the husband tried to push through the fibrous tissue, thus making a tear which can run in different directions, not only along the circumcision scar. The outcome of this may be serious, as illustrated by the case of a 23 year old woman which I encountered in Sennar Hospital. She had been admitted to hospital complaining of vaginal discharge and incontinence. The condition had started with bleeding, and two days later she could not control her urine. She had been married for two months and after six weeks her husband had gone away to work elsewhere. She said that her husband had not yet attained full penetration. Traditions of their tribe (Kawahla) are for the bride to go to her husband every other day from midnight till sunrise.

Examination revealed an offensive discharge and an extensive tear involving the posterior wall of the urethra as far as the bladder and anterior vaginal wall, so that on introducing a finger into the vagina it would pass immediately through the bladder. The tear was repaired by means of an in-dwelling catheter, after a clinical diagnosis of trauma, during sexual intercourse, involving the anterior vaginal wall which had become infected, leading to a large fistula. This woman had come to hospital on her own initiative.

But the physical consequences of an injury are not all. Together with the cruelty of the husband, a woman may as a result find all sexual relations abhorrent. For example, in El Obied I met a young woman, aged 22 years, who had been divorced for five years. She had had intermediate education and had been married to her cousin aged 33 years who had secondary education. Both were Danagla. The bride had been pharaonically circumcised at the age of seven years. For the first week of their marriage her husband had repeatedly attempted to attain penetration, but without success. She suggested that they should consult a doctor or midwife, or even a relative, but he refused, saying 'I am a man'. As he still failed to achieve penetration he bought a razor and cut along the circumcision scar. This was acutely painful for the bride; there was profuse bleeding and she was taken to hospital where the wound was stitched. Her husband was so embarrassed that he could not accompany her. Subsequently she asked for a divorce. The brutality she had experienced at the hands of her husband had made all sexual matters hateful to her. She refused to remarry, having decided that all men behave in a similar way.

The pain inherent to defloration, the subsequent tearing and bleeding, combined with the fact of a severe circumcision that has deprived her of areas crucial to experiencing sexual pleasure (clitoris and labia) all militate against a woman achieving sexual fulfilment. Women are always afraid and need time and patience to attain any degree of sexual receptivity. Of those women we interviewed, 50% said they have never experienced sexual pleasure and simply regarded the act as a duty; 23.3% were totally indifferent, and the remainder either found it pleasurable altogether or only sometimes. The impression received when asking whether or not they enjoyed sexual relations was that their own feelings were irrelevant and the main object was to please and satisfy their husbands.

Almost all the men questioned said they enjoyed their sex lives and that their wives did too. Some of them considered that a woman's compliance with the sexual act and her acceptance of pregnancy signified her pleasure.

The pattern of complications suggest that intermediate and pharaonic circumcisions are almost the same as regards the tissue excised and the aperture left, although complications are more prevalent among those who have been pharaonically circumcised. The sunna type presents considerably less complications.

Before the operation, tension, apprehension and fear are experienced. In this survey, 954 respondents admitted to having anticipated their circumcision with terror. Some had been taken to the *faki* or traditional healer to calm them and allay their fears. The *faki* usually gave them fumigation, or *mihaia* (water with which the *faki* has washed off a Koranic inscription written on a slate) or amulets to wear. But, in spite of their fear, they said they had wanted to be circumcised; they had been prepared for this day for a long time and had been given new clothes and gold jewellery.

The foregoing shows that circumcision is not simply an operation of a few minutes duration after which it is all over, but the subsequent complications exist until the end of a woman's lifetime. Not only are there serious physiological effects, but even more serious psychological ones, which I consider need deeper

study. Some of these are revealed in the answers to questions
relating to sexual relations and the feelings and attitudes of
respondents towards them.

1. *Mihaia*: water with which the faki washes off a Koranic
   inscription that has been written on a slate.
   Bakhat: Koranic inscription on paper which is then burned on
   a charcoal fire. The resultant smoke is trapped under a piece
   of cloth and the patient either inhales the fumes or the smoke
   is distributed around her by movements of the hands.

3. Deinfibulation and Reinfibulation

Deinfibulation*

Deinfibulation performed to ease tightness entails splitting the scar to widen the aperture — in Sudanese Arabic this is called *tasheem* or *masih*, literally easing. When this is performed for the purposes of delivery, however, the whole scar must be incised along its length, and after delivery it is restitched to resemble the original state of circumcision. For widening the aperture the process is performed by cutting the posterior portion of the scar from below and upwards. The length of the incision is determined by various factors; the operators, the indication and the original size of the aperture. *Tasheem* is usually necessary for treating complications found in pharaonic and intermediate circumcision. Table 3.1 shows the main eight indications for decircumcision.

Table 3.1
Reasons for Decircumcision (Deinfibulation)

Reasons	Number
After circumcision: urine retention and difficulty in passing urine	79
At menarche: difficulty in passing menstrual blood	17
At marriage: difficulty in penetration	66
For delivery	1,038
For infertility	7
For infection, vulvar abscesses	35
For introducing a catheter	13
For examination: in abortion, vaginal bleeding	2

* The terms deinfibulation and reinfibulation and decircumcision and recircumcision are used interchangeably; they are simply different terms for the same process.

50

Indications for Deinfibulation

Urinary Problems
Urinary complications occur after circumcision when a pinhole opening only is left, or the opening has closed so that urination is impossible. Decircumcision was done for 30.98% of all urinary complications in the survey (79). The original circumciser is usually called upon to relieve this condition; we found that 43 cases had been decircumcised by untrained, and 33 by trained midwives. The remaining three cases, all from urban areas, were brought straight to the hospital by their relatives where decircumcision was performed by doctors. Trained midwives or doctors decircumcise under anaesthesia, and with scissors or razors. A small incision is made, and then edges stitched seperately to prevent bleeding. Untrained midwives use the same instruments as for circumcision, without anaesthesia. To prevent the fusion of the two sides a piece of a plant called *tundub* is inserted into the

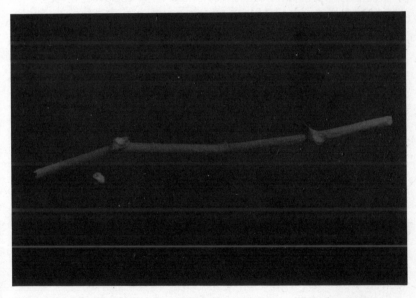

16 *Tundub, a plant used for treating urine retention as a result of tight circumcision by untrained midwives*

urethra, with an end protruding. When the girls wants to urinate, this should be taken out and replaced after urination. This should continue for at least three days. Sometimes the midwife considers that the opening is not too tight, and instead of cutting only inserts *tundub*, a chicken feather, or a piece of soap that has been rolled (called *mashish*); this is left for three to seven days. The wound is washed with acacia to prevent the opening closing up again. This procedure was found to have been employed for 19 of the cases of urinary complications examined by midwives who considered that decircumcision was unnecessary, because a small pinhole opening could be seen. Such an opening is usually so small as to permit the passing of only drops of urine. Decircumcision is needed in such cases, as the following example illustrates.

A 32 year old unmarried women who lived in a village near Medani had been circumcised at seven years of age by an untrained midwife. She was unable to urinate because of tight circumcision, and used to have a piece of *tundub* plant inserted in her urethra, to widen the aperture. Sometimes this is kept in position by attaching it to a piece of cloth which is attached to a tape so that it can be worn around the waist. When she wanted to micturate the *tundub* was withdrawn, and reinserted afterwards. In spite of this, however, she still needed decircumcision, and this was done. Nevertheless, she still needs to spend at least a half an hour attempting to empty her bladder, and before she goes out for any lengthy time she must first spend about an hour to empty her bladder completely. She still experiences severe pain during menstruation and always needs to consult a doctor.

Decircumcision is a painful procedure, but those who have it early are lucky compared to others who do not. It is usually done within the first weeks of circumcision when the girls themselves complain or her relatives notice that she is retaining, or can barely pass drops of urine. But I found many cases where the condition had lasted for years. One woman of 45 years from Khartoum rural area could pass only drops of urine for nine months after circumcision. Her relatives then called in an untrained midwife who decircumcised her with a knife and relieved the condition.

This condition is easily detected in young girls but the real problem is when it happens to an infant, as in the Eastern tribes, who circumcise their girls as young as seven days when, of course, they are unable to complain. When it is noticed that they do not wet their nappies, they are relieved either by inserting a clove, in the same way as the *tundub*, or sometimes by the use of a special type of comb called *khulal*, to raise the skin over the opening to help urination. The woman said that is it known when the child needs to urinate by her crying and hence they apply these techniques.

At Menarche
Here there is frequently a problem in that girls are too shy to complain that they have difficulties in passing menstrual blood. Some do not connect this to circumcision and wait until marriage. The procedure for relief of this condition is the same as that in urinary complications.

At Marriage
Decircumcision usually takes place early on in marriage when the couple experience difficulties in having normal sexual relations due to tight circumcision. 2.3% of cases in the survey had been decircumcised for this reason. It is usually done by midwives (trained or untrained) at home because the couples are embarrassed, or in rare cases an understanding couple may agree to have it done in hospital. The procedures for the operation are the same as for urinary problems. The untrained midwife, instead of using *tundub*, instructs the husband to have intercourse with his wife immediately after cutting, to prevent the wound fusing again. This is painful, but under the circumstances, necessary.

Midwives told me that they are doing a lot of decircumcision for this purpose. One related how a newly married couple came to her late at night accompanied by the girl's aunt. When she examined the young wife she found there was almost no opening, only a pinhole. She decircumcised her, stitched her on both sides and now she is pregnant.

A man from Western Sudan told me that one of his sisters was pharaonically circumcised. On the first day of marriage, her husband failed to penetrate her because she was too tight, he said 'Ma indaha tarig' (she has no passage). He brought a piece of iron to decircumcise her, but she refused. The husband told her family that his wife was too tight, and a group of older women examined her and agreed with him and made two cuts in the circumcision scar. Even then the husband was unable to have intercourse with her. He was very annoyed and eventually divorced her. After some time she remarrried. The second husband also tried and failed to have proper intercourse with her, but a little seminal fluid entered through the tiny hole and the woman became pregnant.

Some men, motivated by male pride, perform decircumcision on their wives themselves (details are given in the section on circumcision and sex).

Delivery

This is the main indication for decircumcision. In fact it must be done for all circumcised cases, whether pharaonic or intermediate, otherwise delivery will not be safe. Decircumcision is necessary for each delivery, and the wound, in turn, needs to be restitched. Trained midwives and doctors use scissors, under anaesthesia for this procedure; untrained midwives do not decircumcise properly, because instead of cutting along the circumcision scar, they make a cut on either side of it. Sometimes, as has been mentioned, more than one cut may be necessary; the untrained midwife as she sits beneath the pregnant woman in the traditional rope delivery, cuts blindly with a knife, without anaesthesia. The wound heals either by binding the legs together as in circumcision, or else it is left to heal by itself; this means that the woman must stay in bed for at least seven days. Sometimes the *gundura* is used, if the wound has not healed after seven days, or some midwives prefer to use the *gundura* immediately after delivery, when it is left for 10-15 days. Oil, acacia, tar and salt are put in the wound to promote healing; it swells then heals and returns to its normal size. The scab formed around the wound is detached with a palm reed. Again either ground acacia, tar or warm oil is poured on the scar. If the woman develops fever it is treated by massaging the wound with oil.

Infection, vulvar abscess

Sometimes decircumcision is necessary in order to drain an abscess. Following this the wound may or may not be stitched. It is usually a small incision done in hospital.

Rare indications shown from the results were:

Infertility: Some couples lived with tight circumcision which was only discovered when they complained of infertility. Decircumcision will be performed only when all other causes have been excluded. In some cases pregnancy followed immediately after decircumcision.

Difficulty in introducing catheter: This occurs mainly in cases of Caesarean section. I also know of a diabetic case, brought into hospital in a coma. Doctors failed to introduce a catheter until decircumcision was done in order to save her life.

For vaginal examination: In cases of bleeding, abortion, and even for women in labour doctors are unable to perform the necessary examination until the patient has been decircumcised.

Whether or not decircumcision should be done for unmarried girls presents problems. Some families will refuse it on the grounds that this will spoil her circumcision, leaving her uncircumcised and not like a virgin which will lead to trouble in the future when she is to marry. Perhaps this is why all cases of tight circumcision were not decircumcised but were left to suffer.

It is quite common for some women to need decircumcision twice or three times: at circumcision for urinary complications; at the menarche, and frequently at the time of marriage, and of course, it is essential for delivery. The results of the sample revealed three victims who had been decircumcised three times; two cases needed it for urinary complication, at menarche and at marriage, and one for urine retention, vulvar abscess and at marriage. Nine victims were decircumcised twice, for urine retention and at marriage. One 45 year old women who lived in Khartoum rural area said she had been pharaonically circumcised at the age of six years by an untrained midwife and had immediate difficulties in passing urine; three days later she could not pass urine at all. The midwife who was called in to see her tried to find a passage with a chicken feather; then the urine came out. The chicken feather was left inside the urethra for seven days and then removed, but still she could not pass urine normally. At the time of menarche she had similar difficulties in passing menstrual blood and it was again necessary for a passage to be made; this time it was done with razors. This unfortunate lady needed decircumcision yet again at the time of marriage when her husband ordered her to do it because he had failed. In addition to these three occasions she was decircumcised for every one of her nine deliveries.

In general, this operation can be considered as one of the complications or effects of circumcision. Moreover, the decircumcision, a wound by itself, is subject to surgical complications, bleeding, infection, failure to heal. So why if this has to be done — why close the passage at all and subject women to the pain and trouble of opening and reclosing?

Reinfibulation: Occasions when Performed

Recircumcision, or more precisely, reinfibulation is called *adal* in Sudanese Arabic, meaning literally 'reconstruction' or making the opening as tight as that of the original circumcision. It is usually done for women who have been pharaonically or intermediately circumcised, and rarely for sunna or uncircumcised women. The most common procedure, adopted by trained midwives and some doctors, is to pare away the edges of the torn scar tissue and sew the new edges together, under anaesthesia. When, rarely, it is done by untrained midwives, they may use thorns or *gundura*, after paring the tissue. This applies mainly to the intermediate and pharaonic types. A rare procedure adopted by a few midwives and doctors, is to take and stitch the loose, redundant tissue around the fourchette. In the fourth method there is no cutting, since this involves only an application of alum paste, which is believed to prevent the skin from becoming loose. The last two methods can be used in sunna and uncircumcised cases.

From the results of the survey I found that, out of 2,276 married women, 1,100 (48.3%) had been recircumcised. It can be done more than once depending on the indication, and is usually done after delivery because the opening widens, but it is not necessary after every delivery and some women do not have it done until after the second or third. Even after delivery the time for the operation differs. 80.6% of these women were recircumcised within 40 days of delivery, though usually it is done within a week or two. The reason for this is to allow time for all the blood and discharge to emerge before the aperture is retightened. Only 5.6% of those surveyed were recircumcised immediately after delivery, and they complained of subsequent difficulty in urination and passing of discharge.

Sometimes the women themselves asked for recircumcision, especially if it is to be done some time after delivery, but in many cases the midwife does it without asking, as one woman told me, 'Yes, I was recircumcised. The midwife did it after delivery. She does it without asking, depending on my condition.' Recircumcision is also done not only after normal delivery, but sometimes after Caesarean section.

As the aim is to tighten the vaginal opening, widowed or divorced women are recircumcised when they want to marry for the second time, in order to appear as virgins. This had been done by 13.6% of the women surveyed; only 4.1% did this routinely at intervals of six months to one year, in order to always be tight. This false appearance of virginity produced by recircumcision is why girls who have premarital sexual intercourse have it done. Thus, rather than preventing immorality, circumcision can encourage misbehaviour, because girls know that they can always be stitched up again. This point is also emphasized by the midwives who perform recircumcision; they said that those girls or women who misbehaved came for recircumcision frequently, at about two monthly intervals, and they paid a lot of money. One midwife told me that such women come 'All the time, in groups of five or six entering my home one by one. After a lapse of two months the same ones come again. I usually stitch them very tightly but still they come again. I cannot think how they open it.' I asked her if they did not get tired of being constantly recircumcised and she said 'No, this is their work. They are like dogs, because they will not stick to one partner.'

Recircumcision usually takes place at home (87.5% of respondents) while 6.3% of respondents had it performed at the operators' homes, and 6.2% of delivered cases were done at hospital — although it is forbidden. Perhaps for this reason we found that some of those delivered in hospital are not recircumcised until they go home. For the unmarried girls, and widowed or divorced women it is almost always done secretly at the operator's home.

Tables 3.2a-c suggest that recircumcision is a new custom and a sign of urbanization, since it is practicsed mainly in urban areas, particularly in provincial capitals such as Khartoum and Medani. One midwife said: 'It is a new custom and is increasing. Even the new generation of women, who have sunna circumcision come for it after the second or third delivery, either themselves or sent by their husband. Even the educated women, who left their daughters uncircumcised will come for recircumcision.' That this is so, can be seen from the survey results that the prevalence is higher among the educated and younger women. Older women were surprised to hear the term, saying that they knew nothing about it as it was not practised by their generation; they said that the wound will tighten after healing by itself. Recircumcision is spreading now because it is a kind of fashion to imitate the educated and urban people. It is not found amongst the tribes of Eastern Sudan, but it is in Northern and Central Sudan.

Recircumcision is usually done by trained midwives (84.3%) which means that they are introducing it into new areas wherever they go. They obtain a lot of money from it and there were midwives who specialized in performing the operation, such as one of those interviewed in Appendix V. She is very vain, and said that there is a common saying in her area that 'A woman who is not

Table 3.2a
Recircumcision (Reinfibulation) by Age

Age in years	Yes		No	
	No.	%	No.	%
Less than 15	—		—	
15-24 year	140	32.1	296	67.9
25-34	493	54.3	415	45.7
35-44	305	54.1	259	45.9
45-54	135	57.7	99	42.3
55-64	26	30.9	58	69.1
More than 64	1	2	49	98
Total	*1,100*		*1,176*	

Table 3.2b
Recircumcision by Residence

Residence	Yes		No	
	No.	%	No.	%
Urban	776	69.3	344	30.7
Rural	324	28	832	72
Total	*1,100*		*1,176*	

Table 3.2c
Recircumcision by Educational Standard

Education	Yes		No	
	No.	%	No.	%
Illiterate	385	31.8	827	68.2
Khalwa	31	36.5	54	63.5
Elementary	362	66.7	181	33.3
Intermediate	158	79	42	21
Secondary	108	60	72	40
Post-secondary	56	100	—	—
Total	*1,100*		*1,176*	

recircumcised by M. [herself] should not consider herself recircumcised' or 'If M. did the recircumcision then the husband should go home early, but if not then he can go as he likes. He will face no difficulties.' She explained that, 'When I want to recircumcise

immediately after delivery, I cut the circumcision scar with scissors
and deliver the baby, and then press hard on the abdomen so that
all the blood comes out. With a razor I roughen the wound downwards and then stitch it. It takes three to four days to heal and I
give the women penicillin. My scar is distinct from that of other
midwives. Even the doctors in the hospital recognize it, when the
women are examined for delivery or abortion.' Midwives admitted
to getting more money for recircumcising than they do for circumcising, with the addition of presents from the husbands.

Some untrained midwives do perform this operation but only a
few (9.4%) compared to the trained midwives. They said that they
had learned because women asked them to do it. Of all the
untrained midwives I interviewed only three recircumcised, and
they had learned to use scissors and do stitching, in imitation of
the trained ones.

It is quite incredible to find doctors doing recircumcision, but
the survey results demonstrate that 4.2% of cases were done by
doctors. One said that he talked to every woman who came to
him for this purpose, explaining the consequences and saying that
it was unnecessary but found that they insisted upon having it
done, so he complies. His justification was that he did it in a
hygenic way and lost nothing by it, on the contrary, he gained
money. But he overlooked the fact that he is acting unethically,
losing his reputation and respect instead of being a model of
enlightenment for others; one can only assume that he is simply
pursuing his own interests. The negative effect of this is that
when we try to convince women that this operation is not necessary, they will immediately reply that doctors do it, therefore, it
must be a good thing. Doctors who perform recircumcision earn
up to £s.50 per case. The following is part of an interview with a
gynaecologist who is against circumcision and has made strong
efforts in this field, but paradoxically is also in favour of recircumcision. He said 'I do not know whether you have looked at
women after delivery, they actually look more like horses than
human beings. If the husband comes and asks for recircumcision
his request is quite reasonable because that is a vagina for a horse's
penis not a man's. It is really very patulous because all the tissues
have been removed; also, following childbirth, the wound may
be infected. Even as a doctor when I see a woman like that I will
ask her to come and be tightened. This does not apply only to
Sudanese women but I found many European women have their
interoitus tightened without having the vulva cut. It needs a small

operation in the fourchette; cut and stitch, you actually end up with building the fourchette.' He went on, 'It is advisable that it should be retightened to admit two fingers, which is wide enough for intercourse. Of course the penis will be much bigger than that but it will widen later on.' When I commented that it is made so small that it cannot even accommodate a little finger, he paused for a while, and answered with 'ya' in a very, very low voice.

As in the case of circumcision the smaller percentage of recircumcisions were done by nurses (2.1%). Maybe because usually they do not circumcise or deliver.

As tradition or custom is the main reason for circumcision, so it is for recircumcision as Table 3.3 illustrates; here also the effects and strength of the tradition is demonstrated. We found that women who had not wanted the operation nevertheless felt compelled to conform with traditions, saying in effect, 'These are our customs and we cannot abandon them.' or 'We will be teased.' [if they are not recircumcised]. However, the role of the women themselves, their husbands and mothers cannot be ignored.

Table 3.3
Reasons for Recircumcision

Reason	No.
Desire to please husband	295
Following advice of mother, mother-in-law, and grandmothers	273
Husband's request	104
Her custom to do so	255
Repair	233
Tradition	337
Ashamed not to have it	161
Fear of infection	55

Table 3.4
Complications Encountered after Recircumcision

Complication	No.
Tight recircumcision	191
Tight recircumcision which needed decircumcision	48
Urine retention	57
Difficult penetration	145
Infection	65
Irregular cycles	9
Difficulty in passing menstrual blood	17
No complication	849

Husbands play an important role here because the second most common reason given in our survey was the desire to please the husband. The women either sought recircumcision themselves or their husbands requested them to do so. Interviews with both women and men clearly demonstrate that men are partly responsible for maintaining this custom. Of the women respondents 88% (881 out of 1,100) said that their husbands agreed to it and 84% (423) of the men respondents wanted their wives to be recircumcised. The women insisted that their husbands wanted recircumcision otherwise they would not have it done, neither would their husbands have given them money for it. Even if we told them that their husbands had said they did not want recircumcision and therefore they had done it by themselves, they would say 'They are liars, bring them here and you will see.' The reason men want recircumcision for their wives is because they think that tightness will result in greater sexual pleasure.

The assumption that men were largely responsible for continuation of this practice is borne out by the following examples: A 39 year old Danagla woman when asked why she was recircumcised said, '*Adal El Rujal*' (i.e. men's recircumcision). When I asked what she meant, she said 'Yes, it is men's recircumcision because women do it for them; it is they who want it.' I enquired if her husband had wanted her to be recircumcised and she said 'Yes'. When I asked how she knew that her husband or other men wanted recircumcision for their wives, she said their behaviour made this clear; they started looking for another woman. 'Looking here and there'. She continued, 'I used to have recircumcision. I had it seven times after each delivery. Once, after one delivery I did not have it done, thinking that the opening was not too much. I noticed a change in my husband's behaviour. He did not talk to me as usual and was increasingly absent from the house. He was always depressed and angry, even with the children. I was very worried and asked him if anything was wrong in his work or the house, but he gave no reply.'

'Talking to my friends one day I mentioned the problem of my husband. One of them asked me when this had started, I said after my last delivery. She asked if I had had recircumcision. When I said no my friend commented that this might be the reason. The following day I went to the midwife to be recircumcised. My husband's behaviour then changed dramatically. He bought me new clothes, gave me more money for household expenses and stayed at home most of the time.'

I once suggested to a woman from the Gezira who always had recircumcision after each delivery, that she might not have it done on one occasion. She totally refused saying 'If my husband rejected me, will you support me? He would not bring me anything, clothes or perfumes.'

Midwives who perform this operation highlighted the husbands' role, saying that they frequently ask them to recircumcise their wives. Sometimes before or during the delivery they will say 'Do not forget your duty' or 'Perform your job perfectly and I will please you', or '*Zabitiha*', (i.e. make it very good). By this it is understood that he means recircumcise his wife without asking her. The midwives receive a lot of money and presents from the husband for this service. One midwife was asked if any men came to ask her for recircumcision of their wives. She said 'Oh yes. Some of them come two or three times and if they do not find me I will go to them. They pay me and advise me how to do it.' She recollected a case when she was ill and a particular women was delivered by one of her colleagues. Forty days after the birth the husband had intercourse with his wife and was very angry and demanded the return of the money he had given her for recircumcision. She said, 'I recircumcised her, eight months after that delivery. Her husband was so pleased! He bought his wife new clothes and presents and talked about it everywhere.'

To another midwife I said 'The women say that the men want recircumcision for their wives, and the men that they do not. What do you think?' She immediately replied, 'The men are liars. More men than women ask us to recircumcise. Even highly educated men; but I will not tell these peoples' secrets or their names.'

Another midwife told of one lady who was delivered by Caesarean section. Her husband (who was an educated man) was very angry and told his wife that she had spoiled everything, because he had been eagerly anticipating her recircumcision. To please him, the woman was recircumcised 40 days after delivery. This midwife pointed out that the many cases of recircumcision after Caesarean section clearly demonstrate that the husband's sexual pleasure is the main motive.

I was also told by one midwife how she recircumcised a woman who had never been circumcised. Whilst she was in El Obied, a Pakistani man asked her to recircumcise his wife. 'I explained to him that she had not been circumcised. He said he knew this but would tell me what to do. So, under his instructions I took the surplus tissue posteriorly from the side and stitched, making the opening tight. I realized this was a better method than our usual one, because as a result of repeated deliveries and recircumcisions, eventually there will be no tissue left. From that time I always use this method for recircumcising Sudanese women.'

4.5% of recircumcised women interviewed maintained that they had not wanted recircumcision, but their husbands had insisted upon it. One woman said that when she had not been recircumcised her husband complained angrily that he had given her everything she had asked for the delivery and yet 'Why do you treat me like this?' She had no choice but to have the operation done.

Another lady from Omdurman said that she was not convinced that recircumcision was necessary but her husband constantly protested that it was. After her second delivery she still refused, and he said he would not longer tolerate it. He sent her home and complained to her mother, who tried to persuade her to be recircumcised. Eventually, unwillingly, she complied, to avoid further problems.

Midwives had many examples of husbands' creating problems. One told of a husband who asked her to recircumcise his wife who had been delivered three times and refused each time to have it done. He asked that this time it should be done without telling his wife. This she did, under anaesthesia, immediately after the baby was born. But when the woman urinated she said to the midwife, 'How is it that I used always to hear the sound of my urine and now I cannot?' The midwife then told her what she had done. When the woman realized what had happened she was very angry, but 'The man was so pleased he gave me a lot of money and presents. Whenever he meets me or on special occasions, he gives me money and presents.'

Another midwife told how, after delivering a woman and, in accordance with her request, not recircumcising her, the husband came angrily to her house saying, 'Why do you leave my wife like this? Go and do your work!' and ordered her to go immediately to his wife and do what he demanded. The wife angrily consented to be recircumcised, saying that he had never discussed it with her. 'Two weeks later, her husband came to my house with lots of presents, dresses and fruit, in addition to some money. Since then I prefer to ask the husband's opinion on this matter.'

Women do not want recircumcision because it is not only painful, but unnecessarily harmful, but if they refuse it can have disastrous results. Educated couples have been divorced because, if a wife persists in refusing, her husband will probably spend his time drinking and with other women whilst continually abusing his wife.

With all these incidents in mind I commented to a group of women 'I do not know what it is that men like about this.' The women laughed, and one of them said 'Why? They are Sudanese and it is their custom.'

Of course, none of this absolves mothers, or grandmothers or even the respondents themselves from blame. I met a 25 year old lady from Khartoum, who after her first delivery refused to be recircumcised. Her mother asked her to have it done, but remembering the horror and pain of her early marital life as a result of pharaonic circumcision she refused, and her husband agreed with her. Her mother said it was shameful and that her relatives and friends would laugh at her, and eventually she refused to eat or drink unless her daughter consented. So the daughter had no alternative except to undergo the operation to save her mother, and hurt herself.

There are other reasons for recircumcision, of which the least acceptable is repair. The women concerned said that as they have already been damaged it will make little or no difference. Those who do not, will not admit to this in order to escape the criticism of society.

As recircumcision involves cutting and stitching, similar complications may be expected to those for initial circumcision. Table 3.4 shows that the main problem is tight recircumcision, which sometimes leads to difficulty in penetration. The results of the survey show that about 48 out of 191 cases of tight recircumcision needed decircumcision. Therefore, why should a woman be recircumcised at all and subject herself to these harmful problems? For example, there was one young woman who, 15 days after delivery of her first child was recircumcised at home, by a trained midwife, only because her mother insisted and said it was shameful not to do so. She thought that the pain and difficulty in urination she experienced would be cured by this. But when she was ready to resume her sexual life, her husband found penetration almost impossible. The only solution was decircumcision. The woman was admitted to hospital for four days for this, but sadly she contracted an infection in the wound and needed to be admitted again. Thus, she spent almost three months in pain, without any justification. In spite of this her mother asked her to be recircumcised after the second delivery, but she said she could not bear even to hear the word 'recircumcision'.

Compliance with this operation really manifests the ignorance of women and their acceptance of a position merely as instruments for men's pleasure. They deny their rights to equality and to have mutual feelings. What is really pitiful is that it is the younger, educated women who do it, when they should oppose, rather than popularize this practice. The most iniquitous aspect is that they set an example which is followed in the name of conformity with the mores of educated society.

4. Attitudes Towards Circumcision

Like other traditions and customs, the circumcision of women does not receive unanimous approval. But those who disapprove cannot say so because the subject is taboo; they dare not stop the practice themselves and thus it continues because there is a sense in which it is assumed it always has existed and, unquestionably, it always will. This was clear from the response to the question 'Why do you practice circumcision?' which brought the immediate, shocked answer, 'Shall we stop it?' (i.e. 'Are you daring to suggest we should not?'). It was, in fact, difficult to define any clear attitude towards the practice.

Out of the total number of women interviewed (3,210) 2,652 (82.6%) favoured the continuation of the practice; only 558 (17.4%) were totally opposed to it. Of those who supported its continuation, 42.9% were in favour of the intermediate type; 28.2% of the pharaonic; 23.5% of the sunna, and 5.4% expressed no particular preference, i.e., they accepted whichever was current practice. Of a total of 1,545 men interviewed 1,355 (87.7%) were in favour and only 12.3% opposed the continued circumcision of women. 73.14% of those in favour preferred the sunna, 18.45% the pharaonic, and only 4.28% the intermediate type of operation; 4.13% expressed no particular preference. It should be noted that the term sunna, when used by men, is somewhat misleading because they tend to think there are only two types — the pharaonic and sunna. From these results it is clear that attitudes are changing; not to the extent of considering that the practice should cease altogether, but at least that less severe forms are preferred.

The proportion of both sexes who opposed circumcision of women is not very high; not surprisingly, the proportion of women who opposed it was higher than that of men. The ratio of

women who supported its continuation was 5:1, and that of
men almost 7:1. Doubtless, this is because it is the women v
suffer most. Nevertheless, of those who opposed the practice. ot
all refused it for their own families; this was demonstrated by the
fact that when asked about their own daughters, about 5.5% of
opposing women and 4.3% of opposing men said that they would
have them circumcised in accordance with the prevalent type in
society at the time. Probably they fear the criticism of society and
are compelled to submit to the immense social pressures which
undoubtedly exist.

Two important factors affecting attitudes or opinions in this
matter are age and education. Table 4.1 clearly indicates that
younger respondents of both sexes were either totally opposed to
any form of circumcision or favoured the sunna. This applies
particularly to the men. When relating type preferred with educational standard, Table 4.2 reveals that respondents with higher
levels of education either totally reject circumcision of women or
accept only sunna; this is supported by previous evidence suggesting
that the type of circumcision preferred depends upon the education of the parents. That the younger and better educated
generation tends to oppose circumcision or prefer the sunna type,
indicates an encouraging attitude among the generation upon whom
we depend to initiate a campaign for total abolition of the custom.

Table 4.3. indicates that overall, the main reasons for approving
of circumcision are: for women tradition, and for men religion.
When reasons for approval are related to type of operation we can
see that: for pharaonic, both selected tradition; for sunna, most
men opted for religion; women said because it is less harmful than
pharaonic; for intermediate, most women selected tradition, whilst
men said it was less harmful than pharaonic. The main reasons for
opposing circumcision were: for women, difficulties during
marriage and problems at confinement, whilst for the men it was
failure to achieve sexual satisfaction.

Reasons Proferred for Approval of Circumcision

Tradition
As the results of the survey demonstrate, tradition was the primary
reason for retention of the practice of circumcising women offered
by women themselves and the secondary reason offered by men. In
a country such as the Sudan, where social pressures are strong,

Table 4.1
Preferred Types of Circumcision by Age (Both Sexes)

Age group (years)	No circumcision (%)	Sunna (%)	Pharaonic (%)	Intermediate (%)	Any type (%)
Under 15*					
Women	0.22	0.44	0.66	0.68	0.06
15-24					
Women	8.79	8.13	7.07	12.9	1.8
Men	3.1	11.78	12.65	0.58	1:23
25-34					
Women	4.48	5.42	6.69	11.4	0.87
Men	5.18	19.16	4.14	0.26	0.59
35-44					
Women	3.27	2.92	4.04	5.89	1.46
Men	2.33	17.6	4.66	0.45	0.45
45-54					
Women	0.26	1.52	2.58	2.80	0.12
Men	1.04	8.87	2.59	1.36	0.71
55-64					
Women	0.2	0.5	1.4	0.47	0.06
Men	0.39	5.11	1.61	0.45	0.34
Over 64					
Women	0.2	6.47	0.59	0.34	–
Men	0.19	1.61	0.52	0.65	0.26
Total % of all					
Women respondents	*17.4*	*19.4*	*23.3*	*35.5*	*4.4*
(3,210)	(558)	(623)	(748)	(1,140)	(141)
Total % of all					
Men respondents	*12.29*	*64.14*	*16.18*	*3.75*	*3.63*
(1,355)	(190)	(991)	(250)	(58)	(56)
Total % of Women favouring circumcision					
(2,652)		23.49	28.2	42.99	5.32
Total % of Men favouring circumcision					
(1,355)		73.14	18.45	4.28	4.13

* Young men in this age group were not included.

traditional practices are taken for granted; it does not occur to
anyone to question them; traditions are complied with because

Table 4.2
Preferred Types of Circumcision by Education (Both Sexes)

Education	No cir-cumcision (%)	Sunna (%)	Phar-aonic (%)	Inter-mediate (%)	Any type (%)
Illiterate:					
Women	2.7	5.1	14.84	19.9	0.72
Men	1.06	13.33	7.96	1.06	2.06
Khalwa:					
Women	0.98	1.32	0.34	0.44	–
Men	0.85	10.4	2.63	0.63	0.21
Elementary:					
Women	5.4	5.43	5.36	9.95	2.52
Men	1.99	17.41	3.62	0.84	0.28
Intermediate:					
Women	3.2	3.8	2.1	2.8	0.43
Men	1.42	8.34	0.49	0.63	0.21
Secondary:					
Women	4.19	3.1	0.66	1.56	0.79
Men	3.55	10.03	1.2	0.42	0.28
Post-Secondary:					
Women	0.88	0.65	–	–	–
Men	3.41	4.6	0.21	0.07	0.21
Total:					
Women	*17.4*	*19.4*	*23.3*	*42.99*	*4.4*
Men	*12.29*	*64.14*	*16.18*	*3.75*	*3.63*

Note: Percentages calculated from total number of respondents:
      3,210 women; 1,545 men.

they are firmly woven into the social fabric. Typical responses to our question, 'Why do you continue to circumcise women?' were on the lines of: 'It is our custom and we are powerless to stop it' or 'Why should we stop doing it?' It is believed that any attempt to abandon such customs would be met by the disapproval of society manifested in ostracism and insults — especially in the case of circumcision; the expression 'son of an uncircumcised mother' is the strongest possible form of abuse.

Other traditions and customs, such as facial scarification and tattooing the lips of women at the time of marriage, have disappeared as a result of education and modernization. The rationale

Table 4.3
Reasons for Choice of Preferred Type of Circumcision (Both Sexes)

Reason	Sunna	Phar-aonic	Inter-mediate	Any	Total
Good traditions:					
Women	116	302	485	11	290
Men	178	167	11	14	370
Religious demands:					
Women	166	111	384	7	688
Men	647	15	6	12	680
Cleanliness:					
Women	82	91	87	30	290
Men	284	42	15	3	344
Better Marriage Prospects:					
Women	9	56	29	–	94
Men	31	14	6	2	53
Greater pleasure for husband:					
Women	9	79	25	–	113
Men	177	53	12	5	247
Preservation of virginity and prevention of immorality:					
Women	36	88	66	–	190
Men	56	4	13	–	109
Less harmful than pharaonic:					
Women	187	–	233	–	420
Men	455	–	29	–	484
Increased fertility:					
Women	7	–	22	–	29
Men	16	3	2	1	22
All these reasons combined:					
Women	18	–	7	100	125
Men	19	–	4	20	43

for continuation of the custom of circumcision of women is, that unlike scarification and tattooing this is performed on a part of the body that is concealed — and about which people do not, or are supposed not to discuss.

This particular tradition plays an important role in some tribes. It is an integral part of the sequence of events in a girl's life especially in relation to marriage. For example, circumcision is considered to be a declaration of eligibility for marriage by the Shanabla tribe. People are invited to attend and the young man interested in marrying the girl also attends the ceremony and afterwards takes the parts excised, digs a hole in the ground and buries them. This is a manifestation of his desire to marry the girl, and on that day formal consent is given. The boy and the girl remain apart till the girl's first menstruation, after which they lead a normal married life. A similar procedure is found among the Taaisha tribe, circumcision is very important. According to one of the midwives interviewed, herself a Taaisha, girls are circumcised at the age of eight years, in the name of a cousin on their father's side; or, if the girl has no cousin, then the man who wants to marry her. The future husband or his father should pay all the expenses of circumcision. The offical marriage sometimes takes place on that day, when the man brings an amulet and gives it to the girl. If no official marriage is to take place the man should not attend. The couple begin their married life, with another marriage cere-mony, when the girl first menstruates.

This midwife herself had her official marriage when she was circumcised, in 1953. The circumcision celebrations for her continued for 15 days and all her relatives attended. Only six years later, in 1959, did she actually begin married life.

In some societies circumcision is considered to be an initia-tion into adulthood. For this reason a girl who has undergone this operation is not allowed to go outside, either to play or even to visit the shops because, officially, however young, her status is considered to be that of a woman. In some societies girls who have been circumcised are forbidden to go to school, because it is thought to be shameful to allow circumcised girls to go out and about freely. These girls must, therefore, remain at home and wait for a husband.

Religion
This is the primary reason given by men and the secondary given by women. This is mainly due to the word 'sunna' which is inaccurately used for one type of circumcision; to say that some-thing is 'sunna' makes it unquestionable for Muslims. Thus respon-dents, especially men, would say 'This is the sunna of the Prophet' or 'We are following our religious teaching', 'We are Muslims'. In fact circumcision is not practiced in all Muslim countries, but when we mentioned this to respondents they said they did not know this. The sunna type circumcision is practiced by some religious Muslim families and by the Rashayda and Misseryia.

Due to its strong influence, the Islamic religion has been used to oppose efforts directed towards abandoning circumcision. In the early 1930s during the Condominium rule, the 'Republican Brothers', a religious and political party, tried to stir up public opinion against the then colonial government's move to ban the practice by maintaining this was interfering in their intimate religious affairs. The issue was mainly political, but they employed this religious approach because they were sure of its effectiveness. But circumcision was practiced long before the advent of Islam, thus it cannot be justified as an article of Muslim faith.

Circumcision of men is referred to in the Koran though not explicitly. The Mufti of the Sudan, Shiekh Ahmed El Tahir, in 1945, (quoting Quortobi's Commentary Vol. II) said that 'Circumcision was practised by the Prophets and the first one to be circumcised was Ibrahim'. Sura II, Verse 110, of the Koran says, 'When his Lord made trial of Ibrahim by commands which he fulfilled'; Sura XVI, Verse 120, says 'Thou shalt follow the religion of Ibrahim, the sound faith'. It is maintained that circumcision is one of these commands and that Ibrahim fulfilled it by being circumcised at the age of 80 years.

Circumcision for men is a tradition, an ordinance and attribute of the Islamic faith. In the Hadith or sayings of the Prophet, Abu Huraira stated that Mohammed said, 'Islam is the religion of purity' and 'Purity is accomplished by five deeds: circumcision, removal of the pubic hair, trimming of moustache, paring of nails and removal of hairs from under the arm pit'.

Circumcision of women is not explicitly enjoined in the Koran, but there are two implicit sayings of the Prophet Mohammed: 'Circumcision is an ordinance in men and an embellishment in women.' and, reportedly Mohammed said to Om Attiya, a woman who circumcised girls in El Medina 'Do not go deep. It is more illuminating to the face and more enjoyable to the husband.' Another version says, 'Reduce but do not destroy. This is enjoyable to the woman and preferable to the man.' But there is nothing in the Koran to suggest that the Prophet commanded that women be circumcised. He advised only that it was important to both sexes that very little should be taken. In fact in Islamic terms circumcision of men is *khitan* and of women *khifad*. *Khifad* literally means 'reduction'. El Nawawi, an eminent authority of the Shafia sect, described the type recommended by Islam as 'The removal of the lower part of the protruding skin at the top part of the vagina' (i.e. the skin of the prepuce). This is typical of sunna proper, where only the excess skin covering the clitoris is excised, leaving the clitoris itself intact.

Circumcision for women is said to be 'preferable', *makrama* or 'embellishment'. That it is in some way related to religion is indicated by the fact that Christians in some societies — Copts, Catholics or Protestants — are known to practice it, as well as some Islamic peoples.

Cleanliness

This reason came third for both sexes. They considered an uncircumcised girl to be dirty and impure because they believed an offensive discharge and smell emanates from the clitoris, which is perhaps why in Arabic circumcision is called *tahur*, meaning purity and cleanliness. Some even said that an uncircumcised girl is not allowed to pray. When respondents were asked why they circumcised their daughters, they said 'We cannot leave them dirty and impure and smelly'. One woman said that men will not eat food prepared by uncircumcised women, and that she could smell the female genitals in food offered by an uncircumcised woman. One midwife, said that she favours circumcision because it covers the genital area, thus preventing it from being contaminated.

Beautification is also related to cleanliness, which is why circumcision is considered as *samaha* or beautification. One woman respondent said 'Circumcision is samaha. *Aad el samaha bitanabi*' meaning, it is beautification, and as such will not be rejected. When a girl is circumcised, they said, she has been made beautiful, because the external genitalia is ugly, especially the clitoris. There is a saying that 'If you look at the womens' genitalia frequently by day you will go blind'. But one man said that up to now Sudanese men did not realize the pleasure and erotic excitement of looking at a naked women. Women are usually ashamed of their sexual organs and cover them. Even wives will not allow their husbands to see them naked; she gets into her *tobe* or under the blanket, then her husband can go and have intercourse with her.

Better Marriage Prospects

This does not seem to be a particularly important reason given by either sexes, yet it plays a part in the continuation of circumcision. It is true that an uncircumcised girl will rarely find a man to marry her, and in Sudanese society where marriage is seen as a privilege for women and for a girl to get married of prime importance, women dare not risk rejection. It is said of an uncircumcised girl, 'Nobody will marry her' 'The bridegroom will send the bride home the same day if she is not circumcised.' Respondents told many stories of men who refused to marry uncircumcised girls or asked their wives to be circumcised or change their circumcision, otherwise they would divorce them.

I was told of a poor girl, from Kassala whose mother had died when she was two years old. Her father remarried and insisted that his daughter should stay with him. He had more daughters from his second wife and, whilst she had them circumcised she left her step-daughter uncircumcised. On the girl's wedding day, her husband, discovering that she was not circumcised, divorced her immediately. He did not dare say why. Of course, people wondered about and discussed this and finally it was remembered that the girl was not circumcised. Her father immediately took the girl to his mother, and asked that she have her circumcised; he also divorced his wife because of her negligence.

Since the men are instrumental in this they should admit it, but from the results of the survey it can be seen that the percentage was the same for both men and women. Perhaps men did not wish to incriminate themselves. The women challenged the men declaring that if men made it clear that they preferred uncircumcised women and refused to marry those who were circumcised they would abandon the practice. But they had found no men willing to do this. One man agreed that if men demanded uncircumcised girls, the custom of circumcision would die out in a generation or two.

Greater Pleasure for the Husband

The belief that circumcision gives more sexual pleasure and satisfaction to the husband was given by both sexes, although it seems that men were more inclined to believe this, as it came fourth for men and fifth for women. The conviction that a tight orifice provides great pleasure for men is the rationale for recircumcision. This assumption is evidenced by the responses of both women and men and also why more than 80% of the couples wanted recircumcision. One doctor commented that when the vaginal orifice is very tight the pleasure for men is more acute but actually of shorter duration, because the tighter it is the more quickly will he ejaculate. They do not know that in a sexually aroused woman the labia majora and minora fill with blood and the tightness which they seek occurs naturally.

Although a tight and narrow vaginal passage makes sex painful for women, they accept this because they think that sexual enjoyment is a masculine right only, and they must do everything possible to please and satisfy their husbands. Some men said they enjoyed intercourse more with circumcised than with uncircumcised women because the uncircumcised women make more demands.

Preservation of Virginity and Prevention of Immorality

This reason was given by 190 women and 109 men. The Sudanese community, being a conservative one, pays strict attention to the behaviour of girls, so any means they consider will protect their girls, or prevent them misbehaving will be employed. As long as it is believed that circumcision ensures virginity the practice will continue. It is said that, 'Circumcision preserves the girl's honour' 'Circumcision is a protection', or 'If we left her uncircumcised she will wander about looking for men, she will be a prostitute'.

The belief underlying this assumption is that excision of the sensitive parts will decrease sexual desire, and the small opening left will make sexual intercourse painful, and thus a girl will fear sexual intercourse. This is a common reason given by Arab nomads, since their girls spend all their time with men, working as shepherds.

Circumcision does to some extent deprive a girl of her ability to enjoy sex, but it does not deter her from its practice because her sexual desire is not decreased. Infibulation can on the contrary, encourage misbehaviour because only recircumcision is necessary to restore an appearance of virginity as we have seen in the section on recircumcision. It is not unusual to find an illegitimately pregnant woman with a tight circumcision. Some midwives refused to repeat circumcision, or pharaonically circumcise sunna or intermediately circumcised girls brought by their relatives because they suspect that they may have misbehaved and become pregnant.

I saw one case of a 15 year old girl brought to Omdurman Hospital by her aunt. The girl complained of abdominal pain and distention. On examination I found that she was in the last weeks of pregnancy, but her aunt refused to accept this; I knew the girl was not married. I called on the Registrar who confirmed my diagnosis, but still the aunt refused to believe it. The Registrar said that she must tell the truth because we would not harm the girl, but would admit her for social reasons, until she was delivered. Eventually the aunt confessed and agreed to a vaginal examination, but to our surpise the orifice was so tight that was impossible. The aunt confessed that the girl had been recircumcised when they discovered she was pregnant.

Recirbcumcision makes the vaginal orifice so tight that a man will assume the girl is a virgin, whether or not the hymen is present, whereas if it is the least bit loose, even if the hymen is intact he will assume she is no longer a virgin. This is mainly why sunna or intermediately circumcised women are sometimes thought to have had intercourse when in fact they are virgins. The blood that should be the result of tearing the hymen membrane, is due actually to the tearing of the stitched tissue. Loss of virginity by an uncircumcised or sunna circumcised girl is easily detected by the rupturing of the hymen, but in the case of pharaonic circumcision a man must penetrate a solid wall and will never know if the hymen is intact or not.

The argument that circumcision preserves virginity and prevents immorality cannot be sustained unless it is assumed that Sudanese women are so morally degraded and sexually promiscuous that mechanical means have to be adopted to restrain them. No decent Sudanese, man or woman, would make this assumption. Such a mechanical device, was employed in Ancient Rome (hence infibulation, derived from 'fibula'); a ring or rings were inserted through the labia majora to prevent intercourse and enforce chastity (belt of honour). Slave girls were similarly treated to prevent conception, as child bearing would impede their work. It is also found in veterinary practice to prevent mares from conceiving.

Less Harmful than Pharaonic
Obviously, this was put forward only for sunna and intermediate circumcision. The fairly large number of respondents, especially men, who did is in itself encouraging, because they admitted that pharaonic circumcision is harmful; meaning the problems inherent in the operation itself, in marriage, and at childbirth. It seems likely that those who agreed on the hurtfulness of pharaonic circumcision can, in time, be convinced that circumcision of women is pointless.

Increased Fertility
This reason was offered by very few respondents; those who did believed that uncircumcised women cannot conceive. I could not discover any reasons for this; it was simply a fixed, irrational idea.

Types of Circumcision Preferred

Of the pharaonic type, tightness is the main objective. One woman said 'The opening must be as tight as possible. This is a usual aim of Danagla and Shygia. They do not want the husband to see the face [attain penetration] of his bride early.' Another woman, whom I asked if she did not agree that sunna is better said 'What is sunna! If one is going to drink water, then his lips will take it first. This is just like a sunna circumcision, or no circumcision. A man first must pass his water [semen] in his thigh and legs. A woman who does not make a man do this is not a woman.' In addition to other reasons those who opposed pharaonic said it is related to Pharaoh and believed that anything related to Pharaoh should not be opposed, 'It is called 'Pharaoh', that means it is bad.'

One midwife said she preferred the intermediate, because the pharaonic gives rise to complications during delivery. Moreover it is done hygienically and with anaesthesia. She considered sunna to be no circumcision at all.

Some women preferred sunna circumcision however, because it presents no problem during marriage and labour; while the men who preferred it did so because of its name; the other reason was that it decreases womens' sexual desire. Others, like the midwife, considered sunna equivalent to no circumcision at all; an attitude inculcated into the younger generation. For example, the mother of a seven year old girl from Sennar, was planning to have the child circumcised later because she could not afford it then. The child, however, insisted upon circumcision immediately or she would not go to school. When asked why she wanted to be circumcised, she said, 'I want to go to school but if I go uncircumcised the other girls will mock me'. I asked 'What type of circumcision do you want?' She said she did not want 'sunnia' (sunna) because it was no good, she wanted 'the other type' (pharaonic). I told her that the girls in her area were sunna circumcised. 'No, they are not,' she said, 'they were circumcised by M. and she never does sunna, she said so herself.' I asked how she would know whether or not she was circumcised with the sunna type, she said she would not but 'the circumcision of the girls in our area is not painful'. She was most insistent upon being circumcised, saying that her father would bring her new clothes, perfume, a plastic mat and a Koranic book, just as was bought for her relatives. When I suggested she should wait and be circumcised with her sisters, she said peevishly 'When will they get older? It will be a long time'. I was unable to convince her that circumcision is unnecessary.

This interview reveals many important aspects regarding attitudes towards circumcision. The girls themselves really influence each other by teasing, and this, in turn, reflects the social influence. It also reveals the knowledge and awareness of little girls about such customs. This child must have heard talk about circumcision which had stuck in her mind. She was confident that the midwife M. did not do the sunna. She does not really know the difference between the types, but she was brought up to believe that sunna is bad and the other types are good, less painful and so on.

We have seen that all circumcisions were performed either at home or the house of the operator, or in private clinics, but when visiting El Fashir hospital gynaecological ward I was told of a girl undergoing circumcision there. I was interested because circumcision is forbidden in hospitals, but apparently this case was for social reasons.

The mother of a nine year old girl was admitted to the hospital for hysterectomy. She was a prisoner accused of killing her husband, and as a result her relations with his family were such that she could not leave her children with them. The child had thus stayed with her mother in the prison and went along when she was admitted to hospital. The woman asked the doctor's permission to be absent from hospital for a week in order to have her daughter circumcised, because at nine years of age it was shameful that she was not. The doctor could not give permission and she asked him to circumcise the child in hospital but he said such operations were never done there and therefore he could not do it. But she wept, saying it was very important; that the girl would be mocked. Eventually the doctor agreed and a midwife performed the intermediate type for the girl in the labour room.

Many who approved of circumcision could give no definite reason for doing so, which indicates that they approved only because it was customary practice and other people do it. Even the many respondents who enumerated reasons why they approved gave the impression that they were doing so parrot-fashion, without really giving any thought to the question.

Reasons for Rejecting the Practice of Circumcision

Here some reasons were related to beliefs of the society and others to the operation itself. Men and women, each gave different reasons based on a masculine or feminine viewpoint.

Table 4.4
Reasons for Rejecting Circumcision

Reasons	Women No.	Men No.
Religious prohibition	114	58
Failure to achieve sexual satisfaction	90	66
Complications during marriage and labour	282	30
Personal experiences	120	—
For human rights and the dignity of women	90	45
Fear of infertility	6	10
Other	54	15

Religious Prohibition
This reason was second in order for men and third for women. It is interesting that religious reasons were offered both for rejection, as well as in support of circumcision. Respondents said it was contrary to the teaching of Islam because it is mentioned neither in the Koran nor the Hadith, and is not practised in many other Muslim communities. The Prophet Mohammed himself did not have his daughter circumcised. Some said 'God created us in a beautiful shape, why should we change it?' or they considered it to be mutilation, which is against the teaching of Islam. They were convinced that it is not demanded by Islam, if it was, then they wanted evidence. The Kinin people of Western Sudan eschew circumcision for this reason as we have seen earlier.

There is thus confusion in the minds of people regarding the true teaching of Islam on this subject. The Koran contains nothing concerning the circumcision of women, neither did the Prophet Mohammed recommend or forbid its practice. However, this obvious importance of religious influences is significant, and this aspect should be handled with caution. The participants of all religious people in a dialogue to examine and interpret Islamic teaching on this matter is needed. In this way it might help to convince a large proportion of the community that circumcision is not a religious duty.

Failure to achieve sexual satisfaction
This is given as the main reason for men's opposition to circumcision and the fourth for women. As for religion, sexual achievement is stated as a reason for approval and for disapproval

of circumcision. The men offering this reason were aware that
each partner should enjoy the sex act for the maximum pleasure
and fulfilment of both. If one does not enjoy, or actively dislikes
it, then the other cannot have pleasure. Circumcision deprives
women of their most sexually sensitive parts, and renders the sex
act painful; thus neither partner achieves real sexual fulfilment.
One man was of the opinion that such frustration may lead to
frequent and increased adultery.

But men who said that circumcision gives them more sexual
pleasure, deny the rights of women to enjoy sex. They are concerned only with their own pleasure. This was stated clearly by
one, educated man who had three daughters. He said that he
opposed circumcision because he knew of its hazards, but that he
had had his daughters circumcised to control their sexual desire.
Another man had divorced his wife because she was not circumcised and was sexually more demanding .

Womens' failure to experience sexual pleasure was revealed by
such remarks as 'What pleasure? We only do it as duty' or 'For
men it may be pleasure; for us it is pain.' There is also some
ambiguity since those who said they enjoyed intercourse really
meant that their husbands did, and that is their aim.

One man who thought that a tight vagina resulted in less prolonged intercourse, and hence decreased pleasure, thought that
many men are excited by a large mons veneris and vulva, and
they will not attain satisfaction with infibulated women. To know
the opinion of women about this however, only uncircumcised
women who are sexually experienced and then are circumcised
could say. Similarly only men who have had sexual relations with
both circumcised and uncircumcised women can express a
reliable opinion.

Complications during Marriage and Labour and Personal Experiences

These were the two main reasons against circumcision given by the
women, and should be given very serious consideration because
they reflect the real feelings of the victims, who know from first
hand experience what it means to be circumcised. We have already
seen in Chapter 2 what some of these sufferings entail.

One young lady from El Obied, said that she would never forget
the troubles she experienced and will never have her daughters circumcised. She had been circumcised three times in two years
because each time her grandmother protested that her circumcision

was not good. She was circumcised first at the age of six, with the intermediate type. Seven days later her grandmother decided that she should be circumcised again because she did not want that type. Unfortunately the wound became infected and she needed to have treatment. Two years later came the turn of her younger sisters. The grandmother said that she should be circumcised yet again, because the opening was big. She had noticed this when the girl urinated. So the poor girl was subjected to the operation for the third time. In addition to all these painful operations she has problems with menstruation and actually needed decircumcision at the time of her marriage. Incredibly we met women who said that as they had suffered and survived, so should their daughters and grand-daughters. This seems to be a form of vengeance, or a psychologically rooted reaction.

One man said that circumcision was undesirable in two situations; one at the time of marriage, when it may result in great shame because in his tribe, it was the custom for about five or seven friends of the husband to hold the bride, since by himself he would not be able to achieve penetration, and it might be a month before a normal sexual life was possible. The other was during labour when the woman suffers much unnecessary pain and cutting.

Human Rights and Dignity of Women
That circumcision deprives women of their most sensitive parts and hence of their natural rights to sexuality, was said by some respondents to be an affront to a woman's human rights and dignity. They further believed that for women circumcision invokes an inferiority complex as they perceive of themselves not as partners but as tools of pleasure. Social development is not possible as long as half the population is subjected to this barbarous practice. Typical comments given by the most educated respondents were 'It is inhuman'; '. . . an extreme insult to women's dignity'; 'How shameful'; 'It makes Sudan seem a barbarous nation. As a risen nation the Sudanese must rid them-selves of all customs liable to reflect badly on their reputation'; 'Sudan cannot claim equality with the civilized world as long as women here are treated in such a way as might disgust animals'; and so on.

Fear of Infertility
This was offered as a reason for opposing circumcision only by a a few respondents. Possibly because people do not know how

circumcision could result in infertility; those who gave this reason
said they had heard that infertility was caused by infection and
tight circumcision; as is mentioned by Shandall (1967).

The Fur and Fallata peoples not only do not circumcise their
women but said they knew nothing about it. Some respondents
said simply that it is an unnecessary operation and several men
said, 'It is only a womans' invention.'

Table 4.5
Reasons Suggested for the Continuation of Circumcision

Reasons	Women		Men	
	No.	%	No.	%
Ignorance of consequences	123	23.3	63	35.0
Fear of social criticism	190	36.0	55	30.6
Midwives make it available	9	1.7	4	2.2
Fear of initiating social change	18	3.4	7	3.9
Ignorance of parents	101	19.1	9	5.0
Influence of grandmothers	82	15.5	10	5.6
Disobedience of the law	1	0.2	1	0.6
Non-enforcement of the law	2	0.4	3	1.7
Lack of government efforts to enlighten the people	1	0.2	3	1.7
Insufficient health education	1	0.4	25	13.9
Total	*528*		*180*	

Opposition to Circumcision: Social Pressures

The important point is not why some people oppose circumcision,
but whether they are prepared to abandon its practice in their
families. The results show that not all those who oppose it refuse
to circumcise their daughters, or, indeed have any intention of
stopping it in their families. Clearly this is due to fear of social
criticism. About 43.6% of those who chose sunna as their preferred type, said that for their daughters they would opt for the
intermediate type or whichever type was currently being performed at the time, i.e. which ever type was socially acceptable.
Social pressures are also reflected in Table 4.5 in which the main
reasons for the continuation of the practice — despite the fact that
so many people are opposed to it; and despite its hazards and
complications — were 'fear of criticism of society' and 'ignorance
of after effects'. Society's influence can be so strong that some

parents resort to cheating. Some I met were totally opposed to circumcision and refused to circumcise their daughters, but were subjected to much pressure from grandmothers and society in general, who began insulting them saying 'Aren't they Sudanese?'; 'Everyone else is doing it, do they think that they alone are educated?'; 'They do not have enough money'. Some girls even ask to be circumcised because all their school friends are. Thus, to conform with both society and their own convictions celebrations are held, guests invited, all the actual preparations connected with circumcision are made, but the operator is instructed only to inject the girl with sterile water and make a scratch, or to apply an adhesive plaster in the pretence that the child has been circumcised. Later, when she is old enough to understand, the parents will tell her all the truth. This technique has succeeded in many cases; but failed in some because the grandmothers and other relatives as is the custom insisted upon seeing the circumcision. When they discovered the truth they either insisted upon having circumcision performed properly, or took the girl secretly to the midwife, or began trying to persuade her to compel her parents to have her circumcised. We also found many instances where the child of parents who had decided she should not be circumcised was taken by her grandmother to have the operation performed while her parents were away.

How to Stop the Practice

The opinions of the fairly large proportion of men and women opposed to circumcision and who would like to see it totally abandoned are of the utmost importance. They are the key persons to suggest ways of abolishing the practice and they should lead the way.

As Tables 4.6a and 4.6b indicate, most respondents agreed on the three way, i.e., legislation, education of women and of fathers'. Women chose legislation as the most important method; men chose the education of women.

Legislation
More than 50% of both sexes who suggested legislation, proposed punishment of both operators and parents because of their joint responsibility. About a third of them suggested punishment of operators only. The rest, especially the women, favoured the

punishment of parents, arguing that parents decide, that the operators simply comply. In fact both operators and parents play a role; parents are responsible because they are the initiators; the operators perform circumcision — which is, in any case, illegal. Some of those interviewed said, 'Yes the midwives should be punished because they perform the operation' or 'Prevent the mid-wives, and then we cannot do it'.

Table 4.6a
Suggested Methods for Eradication of the Practice

Method	Women No.	Men No.
Enforced legislation	288	114
Educational campaigns for women	246	127
Talks to fathers about their responsibility	132	107
Improvement of women's status	114	88
Sex education	54	80
Other	18	5
Total	*852*	*521*

Table 4.6b
Preferred Methods for Eradication of Circumcision of Women

	Women	Men
Legislation:		
Punishment:		
of Parents	186	72
of Operators	253	104
Health Education:		
for Women:		
at Home	231	121
by Radio/TV	158	115
by Medical Personnel	79	40
by Religious Personnel	19	16
by Politicians	—	4
for Men:		
by Radio/TV	78	81
by Medical Personnel	105	60
by Religious Personnel	106	97
by Politicians	17	26

They demanded that the law of 1946 prohibiting circumcision be strictly enforced. For several reasons this law has failed to be effective; its main weakness is that only the pharaonic type is prohibited, a limited restriction which allows so much room for manoeuvre it is virtually no restriction. Who would examine the girls? and if there was machinery to do this and a case of phaaonic circumcision was detected the operator could excuse herself on the grounds of accidentally cutting too extensively. This did, in fact, happen in 1947. The midwife-operator was found not guilty and the judge merely warned her; operators were not punished from the first case but only reprimanded. Another reason for the ineffectiveness of this law lay in that it was legislated by the colonial government, and was opposed because it was thus seen as a political issue. It was difficult to bring cases against those who performed the operation because the girls' relatives would never betray their names, even though their daughter's life might be sacrificed. Doctors and other medical staff were in no position to report any case unless death occurred, since if they did parents would hesitate to take their daughters to them if complications developed. Additionally, since the circumcisers were invariably women imprisonment would be virtually impossible, because imprisonment of women is unknown in Sudanese society.

However, respondents were of the opinion that the operators should be punished by imprisonment and withdrawal of their licences, and the punishment for parents should be imprisonment. Punishment in both cases should be immediate and publicly declared.

Education

Most men interviewed (127 out of 521) opted for womens' education as the most important way to halt the practice, whilst the women put it second. There is a tendency for men to attribute responsibility for continuation of the practice to women and that circumcision is a woman's affair. Women, they said, especially mothers, should be taught about the harmful effects of circumcision. Various methods could be adopted but talks to them in their homes, or over the radio by medical and religious personnel or health educators was considered the most effective. But the primary importance was to ascertain that women are reached in their homes, because the majority are illiterate and rarely go out. Both women and men were agreed on this point.

Education of fathers was put third by both sexes; they were in

agreement that this could be most effectively done by religious
teachers since most of those men who approve of circumcision
think that it is sanctioned by Islam. Men are inclined to see their
role in this matter as a minor one. And indeed our results indicate
that they did not interfere in the circumcision of their daughters
because they think that this is an entirely feminine affair.

The women who advocated education for the men were of the
opinion that they supported the continuation of circumcision; if
not, why did they give them money and presents on these
occasions? Many of the women discussed their daughters' circumcisions with their husbands who agreed to it; thus fathers' do play
a role in the circumcision of their daughters.

Sex Education
Sex education came at the bottom of the list and was suggested by
only 54 women and 80 men. The Sudanese community is conservative, and still does not accept that sex is a subject for discussion. But this need not be an obstacle; sex education could be
accepted as part of general education, and possibly included in
health education, or, introduced gradually in schools after consul-
tation and in collaboration with the Ministry of Education. Some
steps have already been taken in this direction.

Those who suggested that there should be an improvement in
womens' status thought that this could mainly come about through
education and the participation of women in the community.

The majority of respondents were of the opinion that no one
method alone would be effective and suggested that two or three
should be employed simultaneously. This is viable, because many
factors influence the custom and to isolate one and ignore the
others is futile. This is an inherent reason for the ineffectiveness
of the 1946 legislation. Some people say 'Prohibition by law will
only drive the ceremony underground'; or 'Legislation is useless
as long as public opinion does not condemn the custom' or 'To
begin with legislation would not succeed. Effective law must be
either based on customs or conform to what the people perceive
as just or necessary.' Only if the community has first been prepared for and accepts it can legislation succeed. Once people have
been made aware of the hazards of the operation and the leaders
of public opinion have abandoned the practice, others will follow
— as it is really a matter of imitation or fashion.

A few respondents suggested that girls should be allowed to
decide for themselves, when they reached adulthood; at present

they have no role in this. A few others suggested than men should be persuaded to refuse marriage with circumcised girls.

Attitudes Specific to Men

Since the circumcision of women affects half of society, then the other half must inevitably be affected. For this reason a separate questionnaire was designed for men, mainly to examine their role, attitudes and efforts to oppose the custom. We also interviewed some shiekhs, to seek their opinion, or if they played any role in its continuity. But either men are very little concerned with this matter, or they pretend not to be. Some of them totally refused to answer any questions, some were so angry that they drove the interviewers away. Others said 'Go and ask the women, this is not our business', or teased the interviewers saying, 'Go and find some work to do'. Their main objection to these questions was that circumcision is a woman's affair and men ought not to be asked about it. Perhaps, at least superficially, it is a woman's problem, but as the previous chapter showed, going deeper into the reasons for women's circumcision, it was found that fundamentally men were involved. To give their husbands greater sexual pleasure, because of fear that no one will marry them, or as a form of protection from sexual violation, are some of the basic reasons for women undergoing circumcision.

The results obtained from male respondents demonstrate that men do not differentiate between the types of circumcision; they seem only to know of the pharaonic and sunna types, (see Table 4.7) and nothing about the intermediate which they confuse with sunna; hence the majority said that their wives, sisters and daughters were either pharaonically or sunna circumcised; their ignorance is clear if their answers are compared with the prevalence of each type as given by the women respondents. This ignorance can also be detected from their response to the question about recircumcision. More than 80% said that they wanted their wives to be recircumcised, or they had been recircumcised; while at the same time, about 21.7% said that their wives were sunna circumcised. Here the confusion is clear: recircumcision is not usually done for sunna circumcision. Clearly, they meant the intermediate or pharaonic types.

Men seemed very attached to the term or type 'sunna'. They seemed so pleased and enthusiastic when they said that the 'sunna'

Table 4.7
Types of Circumcision in Male Respondents' Families

Type of circumcision	Mother	Elder sister	Younger sister	Daughters	Wife
Not circumcised	1.2	1.1	3.1	1.1	1.2
Sunna	15.1	16.6	18.5	25.1	11.7
Intermediate	–	1.4	2.3	–	0.9
Pharaonic	66.6	70.8	68.3	69.1	78.8
Type not known	12.4	8.2	6.3	–	7.4
Not known if circumcised	4.7	1.9	1.5	2.4	–
All types	–	–	–	2.3	–
Total number	*1,545*	*1,305*	*1,280*	*995*	*1,031*

Note: Percentages calculated from total number of cases in each column.

type was practiced in their families, because they believed it is the best. To me they said sunna in order to appear to be educated and understanding, as it is known that sunna is practised by the better educated Sudanese.

Fathers apparently play a passive role in the circumcision of their daughters. We found that the majority (75%) said that they did not interfere because they consider this to be an entirely feminine affair. Of the remainder, who were less passive, 17.5% said they insisted upon the sunna type for their daughters, and 6.5% the pharaonic. Only 1% of fathers totally opposed circumcision for their daughters. According to the women respondents, their husbands' opinion was sought in 43% of the cases, and of those 50% agreed to have their daughters' circumcised. The daughters of the other half, however, were circumcised in spite of their fathers' opposition. For those fathers whose opinion was not sought, their approval was assumed because they made the necessary preparations.

By adopting this passive attitude, which amounts to tacit approval, men have participated in the subjection of their daughters and sisters to this ordeal, so they cannot escape responsibility by saying it is a woman's affair.

As fathers, men clearly have a responsible part to play in their daughters' upbringing. The men said they pay the expenses of circumcision only as a social obligation and not necessarily because they agreed that their daughters' should be circumcised. The women, they said, will get money from anywhere if their husbands' fail to provide it.

Some fathers said that they had insisted on sunna or no circumcision but their instructions were ignored. This may be because men cannot differentiate between types of circumcision and consequently women do whatever they prefer; but usually, if men firmly insist upon a particular type the women obeyed. Some men demanded that the midwife and the girls' grandmothers swore on the Koran that only a particular type would be performed. In a few cases, whilst the girls' parents agreed that she shall not be circumcised their grandmothers took them to be circumcised without their parents' assent. On occasion a man's insistence that his daughters are either not circumcised or sunna circumcised can have unpleasant results later. For example, pharaonic circumcision may be insisted upon at marriage, and then the necessary decircumcision performed, thus subjecting a girl to three painful operations. Couples have divorced because of violent disagreement upon whether or not their daughters shall be circumcised, or which type should be performed. Men have been known to take their daughters secretly to the grandmother's house if their wives have refused the operation for them. Women have threatened to report their husband's actions to the police when such things occur. All of these severely disrupt family life with all its attendant ills.

Some women are circumcised after marriage, in accordance with their husband's orders. One midwife remembered a man bringing his wife to her after the second delivery — saying that he was Sudanese, not European — and that she was to circumcise her. She commented that circumcision of older women is very difficult because it usually results in severe bleeding, because the mature clitoris is full of arteries and veins, including one special artery difficult to detect.

Sunna is considered as no circumcision by a number of men, as was obvious from responses to the question on preferred type. There have been cases in which, upon discovering his wife has sunna, her husband has demanded that she undergo pharaonic. If the woman refuses, divorce is likely to follow.

As we noted in an earlier chapter, the fact that circumcisions can be repaired leads to ambiguity regarding virginity, in spite of circumcision being cited as a means of preserving this state. Some men who discover their bride has been sunna circumcised and, therefore, is not stitched tightly, accuse her of having had previous sexual experience. This is not only likely to lead to divorce, but to embarrassing court-room appearances and to prolonged ill-feelings between families.

The result of all these potential difficulties is that many women who had originally been prepared to flout convention and leave their daughters uncircumcised, or to choose sunna, have changed their minds and had pharaonic circumcision for their daughters. In view of mens' reactions, and, in the present state of Sudanese society, womens' dependence upon them, this unhappy decision is forced upon women in order to protect their daughters.

Although some of the men said they were opposed to pharaonic circumcision because of its pernicious after effects, at the same time they did not want an uncircumcised woman because, they said, her sexual appetite would be excessive. But they believed that sunna circumcision controls this desire because it involves excision of the clitoris. One educated man who attended our talks in the Babiker Bedri programmes for eradicating circumcision, said that although he opposed circumcision, because of its complications, in his opinion the clitoris must be excised because it may become over-stimulated and create uncontrollable sexual desire. For this reason he had his three daughters circumcised. I told him that circumcision would not control a girl's behaviour but that the standards of morality of the family background would govern this. Moreover, by this act, he was depriving his daughters of their natural, human right to sexual pleasure. To convince him of the importance of the clitoris, I said that it is the equivalent of the penis, and that circumcision is equivalent to penisectomy. He opened his mouth with astonishment, and all the listeners kept silent upon hearing this. But, even though he seemed unconvinced, this is the truth. Another man, at this same meeting, commented that the belief that circumcision preserved virginity was the main reason for circumcising girls, that as this belief is wrong it should be corrected.

In an interview with a man who had been married to three wives, of whom one was uncircumcised and the other two pharaonically and sunna circumcised respectively, this myth of the sexuality of uncircumcised women was repeated. He said he had divorced his uncircumcised wife because, due to her insatiable desire for sex, he had found her with other men. Previously he had been married to a pharaonically circumcised woman with whom he found intercourse very difficult and had needed a long time to achieve full penetration; also she had experienced problems during labour and had needed to be cut in many directions.

His third wife was sunna circumcised; she neither had too much desire for sex, nor experienced pain during intercourse. From these experiences he concluded that: pharaonic circumcision was bad and minimized sexual desire; uncircumcised women 'have desire just like the dog'; and sunna was best, because the degree of sexual desire was reasonable and there were no problems during labour. All of which suggests that men seek only their own sexual pleasure; one man said that the maximum sexual pleasure for a woman is to become pregnant!

Almost all the men who admitted that they agreed to recircumcision of their wives, said the main reason was that it afforded them greater sexual pleasure. It is painful for women but the tightness was exciting for men, which is why it is called 'men's recircumcision'.

Some who opposed circumcision of their daughters at the same time preferred their wives to be circumcised and to do recircumcision, or wanted sunna circumcision for their daughters and pharaonic for their wives. When I commented on this contradiction, they said that it is important for their wives to be circumcised so that they (the men) could achieve more sexual pleasure. Presumably as far as their daughters were concerned they wished to appear as caring, modern and educated people. In this they are following the present trend in society; later their daughter's will have husbands who will make their own decision of the desirable type.

It is evident that contrary to the men's allegation that circumcision is solely 'a woman's affair' they do play a crucial role in the persistence of the practice. The fact that only 12% of all men interviewed opposed circumcision bears this out.

5. The Fight to Abolish Circumcision of Women

Attempts to prohibit the circumcision of women only began in comparatively recent times. Possibly this is because the custom is very old and deeply rooted and also because, like many customs, it was accepted without question, no one dared to examine its malevolent effects or, even it seems, to be fully aware of them.

This custom is mainly practiced in various parts of Africa. Successive colonial governments as far as possible avoided interfering in the local customs of these societies in order to minimize tension. When they did intervene, such as in Sudan and Kenya, they faced a great deal of opposition. Reportedly the fight against circumcision in Africa was begun in Kenya, in 1906, by the Church of Scotland through the medical missionaries in Kikuyu hospitals, this meant that many girls in missionary boarding schools escaped the operation. This continued until 1926 when local action was taken to limit the operation to excision of the clitoris only. This action was also opposed and became a political issue, with the results that some missionary schools lost teachers.

Early Efforts

Sudan faced the same situation. Here the problem was first seriously considered in 1924, when it was brought up by the Director of Intelligence and the Director of the Sudan Medical Services. But no active measure was taken apart from issuing a circular to acquaint District Commissioners with the problem. The chief of the Islamic court suggested that a *fetwa* or religious decree, should be issued, but other religious leaders opposed this, saying that it was already known that pharaonic circumcision was contrary to Islamic teaching; consequently no decree was promulgated.

Additionally, some religious leaders practiced it on their daughters in their own households.

Nothing further happened until 1930, when the Governor of Kordufan noticed an increase in the practice of pharaonic circumcision, especially among the Nubas, and wrote a report to the Governor-General, suggesting that a law against the practice among non-Muslims should be passed. At that time a questionnaire, prepared by the Duchess of Atholl, was received from the British Foreign Office, and distributed to all provinces along with a request for a report on the situation in each province. Following this a full report was furnished by the Director of Sudan Medical Services concerning the evils of circumcision of women, and its extent. The replies to his enquiries that the Governor-General received from different provinces showed that it was practiced, without exception, in Northern and Eastern Sudan, and in the West some tribes among which it was not traditional had begun circumcising their women; a similar situation was found in the South. The administration concluded that it was important to prevent the practice spreading into areas where it had not previously existed. By that time there was some awareness of the problem among the educated and enlightened Sudanese, who considered the practice to be a social problem and stigma on their society.

In the late 1930s, a British Member of Parliament attacked the custom and urged the colonial administration in the Sudan to take steps to prohibit it by law and warn against proliferation of the practice. This was the first time it had been openly discussed, and it led to the subject featuring widely in the British press and in medical journals. In Sudan the British administration and enlightened Sudanese discussed the matter with extreme caution because any prohibitive action could be interpreted as direct interference in Sudanese affairs, or as a means to divert the attention of Sudanese from the more vital issues of social and political reform. The general attitude was anti-legislation and pro-education since it was thought preferable for officialdom to remain in the background.

However, a movement led by the wives of high ranking British officials who had had the opportunity to mix with Sudanese society and study its customs, began openly discussing the matter, and, with the co-operation of educated Sudanese men, campaigned vigorously against circumcision of Sudanese women and for its abolition generally. The issue was discussed in social clubs and the

93

custom of circumcising women was declared to be outrageous. The resulting social atmosphere became so tense that the colonial administration was forced to seek a solution to the problem.

Their particular concern was centred on the South, and, additionally, they were anxious to prevent the custom spreading. Southern Sudan Governors permitted Muslims to practice the sunna, whilst pointing out its dangers and needlessness, but if it was found to be practiced by non-Muslims it was classified as mutilation and grievous hurt, and dealt with under Tribal Law. Operators were to be punished, and as part of the effort to restrict the spread of the custom the Jellaba, Fur and Fallata were sent to Darfur. This policy was, to some extent, successful.

In 1943 a campaign was initiated, and in 1945 the Governor-General of Sudan published a report by the Sudan Medical Services condemning the circumcision of women. This document was signed by nine members of the Medical Services. In the foreword, the Governor-General stated that he had requested medical officials to prepare the report in order to publicize the dangers inherent in the circumcision of women. This was followed by a statement from the Mufti of the Sudan, Sheikh Ahmed El Tahir, who clearly indicated that Islam was opposed to the custom. Two other statements, one by El Sayed Ali El Margani Pasha, head of the Khatmia sect, and the other by El Sayed Rahman El Mahdi, head of the Ansar sect, both condemned the custom, encouraged the spread of the movement opposing it and pleaded with their followers to do likewise.

Descriptions of the operation and its effects and causes were also contained in the report. In conclusion, all Sudanese were urged to take every possible step to abolish the custom.

Unfortunately, this report was inaccessible to the majority of Sudanese, particularly the women who, being illiterate were unaware of its existence. School mistresses endorsed the contents and signed a pledge to follow its recommendations. They played an important educational role in fighting the practice. One of them, Sit Malka el Dar travelled all over Kordufan Province to urban and rural areas, villages and nomad camps, explaining the harmful effects of circumcision and encouraging the people to stop it. In spite of many obstacles she continued to believe strongly in her mission and insisted on continuing her work.

Legislation: 1946; and Later Efforts: 1975 to Present

In 1946 the British Administration issued the following amendment to the Sudan Penal Code of 1925:

> Unlawful circumcision:
> 1. *Section 284 A(I)* whoever voluntarily causes hurt to the external genital organs of a woman is said, save as hereinafter accepted to commit unlawful circumcision.
> Exceptions:
> It is not an offence against this section merely to remove the free and projecting part of the clitoris.
> 2. Whoever commits unlawful circumcision shall be punished with imprisonment for a term which may extend to five years or with fine or with both.
> 'Explanation': A woman can, by causing hurt to herself, commit an offence under this section.

As we have already observed, the weakness of this law is that it forbade only one type of circumcision; further it was passed before people were prepared for it, which led to incidents such as those in Rufaa, a town in Gezira province, where the first case was brought. The police lodged a complaint under the new section 284 A(I) against a midwife who had performed an unlawful circumcision, and against the mother of the child as an abettor of that offence, and obtained a warrant for their arrest from the local Magistrate. This took people by surprise, especially as the accused persons were women. Demonstrations followed, in which the Republican Brothers played a great part, using the legislation as a political weapon against colonial rule. This led to minor amendments being made to the law, such as the referral of the case to the Governor for his sanction, or the case being transferred for trial elsewhere if proved to be impossible for it to take place in the area where the case had occurred. But few other cases were reported or punished following the Rufaa case; and, as we have seen midwives soon found ways to get round the law.

A more serious effect of the law was that all the people who heard about it, took their daughters secretly at night and had them circumcised before the law came into action. This was called 'bean's circumcision' '*tahur El Fasolia*', when the girls were circumcised collectively, and secretly without any ceremonies. The Beja interpreted the law as unwarranted interference in their social customs and took their girls away to the hills to be circumcised.

Although initially cases were regularly reported under the law this gradually ceased and nowadays one never hears of any trials for circumcision, except if a complicated case is reported and the name of the midwife given. In this event the midwife will be punished locally by the health authorities, the Principal of the Midwifery School and the Assistant Commissioner for Health in her area. She may be warned or her licence withdrawn, but these cases are very rare. Although people were afraid when it was first enacted it turned out to be only a 'paper law'.

In 1947 a national committee, the Committee for Fighting Female Circumcision, was formed, with members from various social and professional categories but only one woman member. It held weekly meetings to follow up efforts for the fight in the field, to make suggestions, and report cases, but eventually it became inactive.

Efforts to abolish circumcision gradually ceased. People became more concerned with political matters, and only sporadic efforts were made. In the capital a very small number of families either stopped circumcision altogether or had only the sunna type performed. Doctors advised their friends and relatives and gave public lectures or seminars supporting the abolition of circumcision; religious leaders wrote articles or gave talks on the same theme, but their efforts lacked systematic organization. Because operators were not punished they were free to perform the pharaonic type, and it appeared that instead of dying out, circumcision was flourishing. Even the educated families continued to do it. In 1977 an attempt at an organized approach to the problem began when it was extensively discussed at the Fifth Congress of Obstetrics and Gynaecology. Different views were put forward and delegates from Somalia participated in the discussion, explaining the situation in their country. As usual recommendations were endorsed but no action followed. A seminar was then held by the Sudanese Medical Students Association where the matter was discussed for the whole evening, but again no action followed.

By this time the subject was a matter of international concern and several organizations and institutions had become aware of it. This led to a seminar in Khartoum in 1979, organized by the World Health Organization (WHO) in which the circumcision of women was the main topic for discussion. Important recommendations were endorsed, stating the need for an explicit policy for abolition of the practice — as usual these recommendations were not followed up. WHO's policy is to assist or intervene only when

asked by government, but while the Sudanese government
approved the recommendations they took no further action.
Government policy is to eschew direct interference in social
customs in order to avoid problems. It cannot, therefore, initiate
abolition of circumcision but only support the efforts towards it
indirectly. This is what happened through the Babiker Bedri
Scientific Association. This body — founded after the Ahfad
Symposium on 'The Changing Status of Sudanese Women' in
1979 — took responsibility for following up recommendations
from the Symposium, one of which was the abolition of female circumcision. The subject was widely discussed in the symposium by
different groups.

As a result, in 1979, a preparatory, or steering committee, was
formed from various national bodies whose terms of reference
were to explore ways towards the eradication of women's circumcision. The first step agreed upon was a national workshop, to be
held in March 1981, with representatives from all voluntary organizations and various official bodies. Fortunately, many representatives from different regions were able to attend; with all the
Principals of midwifery schools, midwives, educationalists,
mothers and mothers-to-be, gynaecologists, psychiatrists, sociologists and religious leaders attending. After a three day discussion
in which the various views were put forward, recommendations
were agreed. Specific recommendations were put forward for
implementation by; the Ministry of Health, Ministry of Education
and Guidance, The Higher National Council for Religious Affairs,
The National Council for Social Welfare and Development, The
Ministry of Culture and Information, Women's Secretariat and
Sudanese Womens' Union, The Family Planning Association, The
Welfare and Youth Training Centre, and the Medical Council. Also
at a plenary session it was agreed that they would all sign a pledge
undertaking not to subject their daughters to this harmful
practice. A national standing committee was then formed from the
steering committe to follow up these recommendations.

The government did not declare an explicit policy or enact a
law to eradicate circumcision, but this support for the recommendations of this body is manifested by the fact that the Minister of
Health was committed to ensure the adoption of these recommendations; the Minister of Culture and Information directed the
media to give all possible help and co-operation, and to permit the
Association to use any of their facilities. The National Council
for Social Welfare co-operated directly, as did the National

Council for Religious Affairs, who provided religious leaders to clarify religious opinion, either in talks or in seminars, in mosques or social clubs. The Sudanese Women's Union, through its different branches in various regions committed itself to instructing its members on this subject and to co-operate closely with the Association. The Ministry of Education agreed to provide sex education in schools which would include information about circumcision. They also agreed that information about circumcision could be included in the curriculum for all levels of education.

The Babiker Bedri Scientific Association is now working with the full support of the Government through the bodies it concerns. Following the workshop, a plan of action was set out. It was agreed to start with an intensive publicity programme on radio and TV, and at the same time there should be direct talks and open discussion with the people where they live. There is now a weekly programme on the subject on the radio and TV, with speakers from different groups, mainly those who participated in the workshop.

In the three towns and nearby villages of the Gezira, we have started to give weekly lectures. To our surprise these lectures are very well attended by both sexes and different age groups, from children to grandmothers. A good sign at these meetings is the participation by all in the discussions, and enquiries about unclear points without any shyness. Questions relating to sex or concerned with personal experience are asked quite frankly. This, in itself, is a progressive step, as even to mention such matters used to be considered impolite and social unacceptable. The more people hear and talk about it, the more will they be aware of the existing problems and think about them. One reason why this practice has continued for so long is that it was not a subject for discussion. It has been proved by experience that, if you want people to give their attention to a particular issue, encourage them to talk about it and they can make their own judgement.

This publicity resulted in a new type of behaviour and response. Children, watching the TV, hearing the radio or attending lectures were made aware of the problem and its effects. They tell their parents that they do not want to be circumcised, referring to these talks. I know personally of many girls who have refused to be circumcised. Some of their mothers came to me saying 'You have done a great harm to us. Our girls refuse to be circumcised because of your talks' 'You have spoiled our children. What can we do for them now?' Some girls hear of the campaign from their friends at school and tell their families. This response emphasizes the importance of starting to teach at the primary levels and the importance of enlightening children.

The response of women when discussing and enumerating the medical problems was astonishing. Some commented 'You are right. We have such complaints but did not relate them to circumcision.' 'We have been circumcised but we will not subject our daughters to it.' And, more importantly, they asked for more information. On the other hand some knew of its ill effects but could not contemplate abandoning the practice; others were not convinced that circumcision was bad. But the fact that they are prepared to listen is itself useful, because in time they will become convinced.

There has also been a varied response among men. But the important point was that they began to understand the exact meaning and distinction between different types of circumcision. Being less shy, they talk about sex more freely, from their personal experience, or discuss why they support continuation of circumcision for women. They also realized that they have a role to play in this.

Some of the talks were attended by midwives who argued that they only performed the operation because they were asked by the people although they themselves do not want to. They were aware of the complications and perform only the sunna type. Two of them made it clear at meetings that they would not circumcise any more and requested people not to come to them for circumcision.

Often, people who heard of our activities asked us to give similar talks in their areas. To some extent these talks were organized according to these requests.

Besides these on-going efforts there is a plan for model areas where a pilot project can be started. The plan is to concentrate on a village or a sector of a city, and carry out an extensive campaign against circumcision there. This will be in the form of lectures, direct talks and field trips. After two years there will be an evaluation of the work: how the people responded, who stopped the practice and why. From these results and the experience gained, a similar programme could be organized in other areas. A programme is at present underway as part of other projects in the White Nile area. Women and men from this area participated in the workshop and were convinced that circumcision of women should be abandoned.

Suggested Steps to Secure Abolition

That this custom has been practiced by almost all Sudanese for a
very long time should not discourage those who are trying to
abolish it. Also, the belief that it is not a health problem, or a
problem at all; that its effects are exaggerated or that it is not a
vital issue for women who struggle hard to survive and feed their
children, should be corrected. It is a problem. It is also true that
there are many problems to be solved in Sudan: medical, social,
political and economic, but this particular problem has a wide
impact, so that all efforts to abolish it should be encouraged. At
least if we solve this problem the total number of problems in
the country will be reduced.

The Dimensions of the Problem

The results of our survey show that circumcision of women is a
deeply rooted custom with all that this implies. It has traditional,
religious, social and cultural sanction and background. Any
attempt to change, or to abolish this custom, needs a very careful
approach keeping all these factors in mind. So the support and
participation of all concerned parties, educationalists, health
personnel, sociologists, religious leaders, politicians, respected and
influential individuals and the public at large is the first and
critical step in the change. In addition, it must be realized that this
custom cannot be stopped suddenly; it needs time, maybe genera-
tions, in order to convince the people and persuade them all to
stop practicing it. There may be trial and failure, but the process
should be continuous, regardless of failure or success at the
beginning.

Education

The main problem in the Sudan, as in many other developing
countries, is illiteracy. The overall illiteracy level in Sudan is about
80% and even higher among women; so I think an important step
in attacking the problem is to provide minimum education for all.
Education will raise the intellectual standard of the community,
and make it aware of the facts and able to understand them.

In addition to general education, a course on sex education
should be included in the curriculum, which should start from
basic facts, such as the anatomy of the genital organs, their
functions and importance, and the similarity as well as the
differences between the masculine and feminine sex organs. It

100

should include information and explanation on how the circumcision operation is performed and what is excised. The results and dangers of the operation itself, the effects of the absence of the parts excised and the harmful consequences should be factually presented.

At present educationalists and policy makers can participate by encouraging the inclusion in present curricula of such instruction, if not as a separate subject it could be included in biology syllabi. Presented in this way the information is more effective than occasional lectures or seminars conducted by specialists. The results of our survey and discussion with people revealed an ignorance of the hazards of circumcision, or that it could result in such problems; they believed it to be a useful process with no ill effects. Not only people's ignorance but the absence of any effort by health educators and others is reflected here. The role of health education and health educators, which at present they do not fulfil, is paramount. As well as disseminating all the relevant information about circumcision, if possible to everyone, they could perform an important service by clarifying the facts of chastity. Parents should be convinced, by anatomical and scientific facts, there there is no relation between virginity and circumcision; that this mechanical seal will not prevent a girl from misbehaving, but the morality and atmosphere of her family. This should be expressed in simple language, taking into consideration the illiteracy of the majority. It should also be designed to suit children, school children, women, men, urban, rural and nomadic peoples.

Use must be made of all the available facilities, with more use of mass media, particularly radio which reaches almost every home as well as television and the press, to create awareness among the people. Again the important point is that this should be a continous process.

Legislation

The fact that legislation against the practice already exists and has failed does not necessarily mean that one should not try again. Perhaps the mistake was in the way it was designed or approached. There must be continuous experiment to attain the desired effect.

It was suggested that some modification of that law might help. The new one should outlaw all types of circumcision — not only pharaonic — and the excision of any part of the external genitalia with the intention to perform circumcision. Punishment for infringement of the law should not only be fine or imprisonment, but action should be taken against the operators and the parents or whoever took the decision to circumcise. In my view, punishment for the operator should be withdrawal of the licence to work in addition to imprisonment for at least five years; punishment for the parents should be imprisonment. Also, the victim should no longer remain in the care of such parents, or others, because by subjecting them to this illegal and inhuman practice without their consent, they clearly are unsuitable to have charge of children. Consent is a very important point even in medically indicated surgical interference, so it is even more vital in this issue.

These punishments should be inflicted from the first known case of circumcision — not necessarily a complicated one, which should be reported immediately. For the trial to be fully effective it should take place as soon as possible after the culprits have been reported and apprehended, and their punishments should be made public; no appeals should be accepted. Social custom dictates that the operator's name should not be given but this need not hinder the trial; it can be discovered from many sources, or, as a last resort, the parent or whoever else is responsible should be imprisoned until they reveal the name.

This law should be immediately enacted by the People's Assembly Council. In my opinion this would not be difficult, and such a law would be readily accepted because the existence of the present one is already widely known, and what I am suggesting is simply a modification or amendment to it. Because there is a general awareness of the problem, people are fully prepared for an official intervention of this kind. Wherever we went during the survey we were asked if the government wanted to stop circumcision. It seems, therefore, that the time is ripe for enacting such a law, and that in combination with other measures, such as education, it would now prove to be effective.

Religion

Religious influence is very important in Muslim Sudan and anything related to it will be taken seriously. Thus, this is potentially one of the most effective channels of communication. We have seen that the circumcision of women is practiced by many families because they believe it is sanctioned by Islam, conversely we have also found that no evidence exists in the Koran or elsewhere to bear this out.

It is thus the duty of all religious leaders, starting with the Mufti or Grand Guadi, and the duty of the National Council for Religious

Affairs to clarify the teachings of Islam on this matter. Their findings should be communicated to the public as widely as possible, in co-operation with other lecturers, in open talks, on the radio and on television. The sermons given in the mosque are another important means of communication even though the mosque is mainly for men. Religious leaders must agree on the correct interpretation of Islam's teachings in this respect and eliminate the present ambiguity which has created so many problems. To maintain that circumcision of women is opposed by Islam while, at the same time, it is practiced by the families of some religious men, or to say that the milder form is sanctioned by the Koran is not conducive to abolishing the practice — rather the contrary.

Because the word 'sunna' implies that this form is recommended by Islam it should no longer be used for the particular form of circumcision to which it refers. Part of the Mufti's duty is to explain to religious leaders that in the true teaching of Islam there is no mention of a so-called 'sunna' operation. Moreover, the fact that it is not practiced in all Muslim countries (Saudia Arabia is one example) surely indicates that in Sudan the Koran has been either misinterpreted or deliberately manipulated. The Prophet's daughter, Fatima, was not circumcised, and it is to be assumed that if the Prophet had enjoined this upon women then his own family would have conformed. Since we follow the tradition of the Prophet, why should we stray from his teachings on this point?

Faki's and sheikhs (religious leaders) too, have an important part to play once they are convinced that Islam does not demand the performance of this operation. Many people, in both rural and urban areas, believe that the *faki* possesses supernatural powers; they consult him when they have problems or fail to have children and always obey his instructions because they believe that whatever he says is correct. They could thus perform a vital service in helping to abolish the practice.

Social Responsibility
Men, have the opportunity to read and to mix with the people outside the family and thus are better placed than women to learn the facts about circumcision. They should see communication of this information to those members of their families who lack the same opportunity as a duty, and their position in society would ensure that their words would be effective.

As husbands, or future husbands, they should make it clear that circumcision is not as attractive to men as women have been led to believe. It is they who know whether or not circumcision enhances their sexual pleasure. If, in fact, they prefer uncircumcised women they should speak out.

As fathers, and heads of the family, men claim total responsibility for decisions regarding what is desirable for their families in almost every aspect of their lives. They expect — and indeed, receive — total obedience in relation to their wishes and instructions within the family. Why, then, in the crucial matter of circumcising their daughters' do they disclaim responsibility and say, 'It is a woman's affair'?

As the most educated and influential members of society men should realize the vital role they can play in stopping this inhuman practice.

The operators — mainly midwives, both trained and untrained — are key figures in perpetuating the practice. They must be convinced of its harmfulness, quite apart from its illegality.

The technique of performing circumcision is not part of the curriculum of midwifery schools, but trained midwives soon learn how to perform the operation. In practice, trained midwives are not forbidden to perform circumcision, but only forbidden to use any instruments or drugs issued to them for their legitimate work. This implies that, to a great extent, their activities in this respect are performed with the tacit approval of officialdom. Midwifery training should specifically forbid the performance of any type of female circumcision. The harmful effects of the operation must be strongly emphasized. Medical ethics should be included in their curricula, and, too, their position vis-à-vis the law, and the punishment for transgression of this law should be made unmistakably clear.

Traditional midwives make up the highest percentage of operators and should be approached in several ways. They could be contacted indirectly, for example when they are helping with deliveries or doing circumcision, and, in a general talk, told of the hazards of circumcision. This should be the responsibility of educated women and women's organizations in their area, who should take every opportunity to meet them and discuss the issue in a simple way.

The potential contribution of untrained midwives should be harnessed and they should be enabled to work under more acceptable conditions, which would not only benefit them but their community. We must first assure them that no action will be taken against them by the government, providing they are prepared to be directly supervised by the local authority, such as health visitors or medical assistants, who should visit them regularly and teach them public health and child welfare practices, and about the harmfulness of circumcision.

In this way they will become useful members of the community and less inclined to hide themselves. A further beneficial effect will be an increased number of trained midwives, and eventually, untrained ones will become unacceptable to the community. But if we neglect them and continue to pretend they do not exist we are doing a disservice to society, because they will continue to work in secret with the consequences we have already described.

Doctors, above all surely know well the hazards, the harmfulness and the many adverse consequences of the operation and should never consent to perform it. Rather than connivance in transgression of the law, they should set an example to society by publicly condemning the practice. Any doctor who performs such an operation should be forbidden from practising medicine thereafter.

The circumcision ceremony, where money and gifts are given to girls is an incentive for the children themselves to demand to undergo the operation. This custom applies to boys as well as girls and in Sudanese society money is given either to the parents or the boys who are to be circumcised. The fact that circumcision of boys is a minor and necessary operation, entailing the excision of functionless skin only and is medically indicated, whilst the circumcision of girls is a major operation entailing the excision of vital parts of their sex organs — a deliberate, functionless mutilation in fact — should be frankly explained to children as soon as they are old enough to understand.

Economic aspects: No doubt circumcision operations provide a source of income, especially for midwives, although to those few doctors who perform this operation it provides only a supplement to their basic income. But for midwives it seems to be the primary and most lucrative source; therefore it is essential to provide an alternative. This could take the form, for example, of: 1) Inclusion of midwives into the pensionable services, since a common complaint is the uncertainty of their future; 2) payment of an improved monthly salary; 3) training to participate in other, related areas, such as family planning, health education, adult education, community development projects and so on.

Community programmes: The struggle to abolish circumcision should be integrated into current community programmes, especially those in rural areas. This will not only disseminate information and raise awareness in the community, but also be an economically viable use of time and money by extending the areas covered by already available facilities. Primary health care programmes are ideal, because they are to be found everywhere, even in the most remote rural and nomadic areas. One function of the community health worker in community development is health education; to this should be added teaching about the hazards of circumcision. The family planning centre and services have, so far not played any role in the eradication of this custom, although their contribution could be most valuable. Those who attend — mothers and mothers-to-be — represent an important sector of the community. Instruction is already provided on matters related to maternal and child health, and the opportunity must be taken to extend this to instruction on the evils of circumcision.

From all that has been said, it is clear that one method alone will not produce the desired result of abolishing the custom of circumcising women. To have the maximum effect the methods suggested must be simultaneously employed in an integrated campaign. The committee already existing under the aegis of the Babiker Bedri Scientific Association could form the nucleus for the formation of a national standing committee representing all the bodies concerned to achieve the abolition of this custom.

Such a committee should embark on a national, organized publicity campaign, with the purpose of arousing awareness of the ill effects of circumcision; providing facts and figures and exposing all the erroneous beliefs about the practice, traditional, religious, social, medical and so on. All channels of communication should be involved, for example: 1) Public lectures, in schools and social clubs 2) Articles in newspapers and journals 3) Interviews and talks on radio and television 4) Discussion groups 5) Publication of pamphlets 6) Children's books 7) Plays, either in theatres, on radio and television and performed in rural communities. These activities should be evaluated after a period of time, both to examine the effects and make plans for the future.

It is hoped that the efforts of such a committee would encourage policy makers to adopt a clear, definite stance which will add strength to this campaign.

Appendixes

Appendix 1
Methodology Employed in Survey

Area of Study

In the original plan all the six former provinces of Northern Sudan were to be covered. However, as noted in the introduction only five out of these six provinces were surveyed, with the Southern region excluded. The provinces surveyed were: Khartoum, Blue Nile, Kassala, Kordufan and Darfur, and both urban and rural areas were involved for each province. The units used were the village council in rural areas and the quarter council in urban areas.
   A multi-stage sampling technique composed of three stages was used:
Stage one: Selection of village and quarter councils.
Stage two: Stratification of councils into segments.
Stage three: Selection of households.
   Stages one and two employed probability proportional sampling, where the selection in each unit depends on probability reflecting its weight. In the third stage, simple random sampling was used: households were listed, then selection took place randomly. The individuals studied included women and men. Men were included mainly to discover their attitudes towards circumcision and their role in it. The sample for men is half that for women.
   One female, ten years of age or more, was taken at random from every household, and one male above 15 years taken randomly from every other household.
   The sample consisted of 3,210 females and 1,545 males divided as follows:

Province	Females	Males
Khartoum	782	386
Blue Nile	1,039	502
Kassala	688	325
Kordufan	338	162
Darfur	363	170

The total sample for females is about 9.4% and for males is 4.52% of the households.

108

Data Collection and Application

Separate questionnaires, for females (form 1) and for males (form 2) were used for data collection (see Appendixes II, III and IV).

Questionnaire for Females
This consisted of two sections. Section A, to be administered to all the respondents, while section B was for co-operative respondents only. The information in section A included: personal identification, medical information, events accompanying circumcision, special questions for married respondents and opinion on circumcision. Section B included: more details of the circumcision ceremony, sexual life and opinion on circumcision.

The Questionnaire for Males
Like that for females this consisted of two sections: section A was for all respondents and B for co-operative respondents only. The questionnaire was more or less similar to that for females regarding, personal identification, sexual life and opinion on circumcision, with more details, especially of types preferred for daughters and wives.

Interviewers of both sexes were involved in the exercise. The team consisted of a medical doctor, social workers, medical, and other college students. The number of interviewers varied from 6-12 per trip, usually one third of the number were men. They were given training for two weeks in how to fill in the questionnaire and how to ask the sensitive questions, in order to ascertain that they conducted the questionnaire satisfactorily.

The output for a single man interviewer was 8-12 forms, and for a single woman interviewer 5-10 forms per day. The average time for the men was 10-30 minutes and for the women 15-40 minutes.

Interviews usually took place during the day time. For women this was no problem because they were usually at home except for a small percentage who were working or studying; they were covered by a later visit. But the men usually left their homes during the morning hours, so male interviewers had to do their work in the afternoons. In the rural areas, where the majority are farmers, both men and women, were usually out of their homes during the day time and had to be visited in the early morning or late afternoon.

I obtained additional information from the midwives (trained or untrained) and other health personnel by interviews and discussions regarding the prevalence of the practice and common complications in their areas. I also visited hospitals to interview anyone suffering from complications there.

At the end of each working day the group gathered to discuss the relevant and important points and problems encountered during the day in order to make plans for the following day.

Before starting the survey a letter was sent to the Assistant Commissioner for Health, to inform him of the purpose of the

study, the date of the trip and to request his assistance in
obtaining lodgings and transport. Also, community leaders, such as
sheikhs or heads of the village councils, were approached to ensure
their co-operation and that of their people.

Questionnaires: 1) Women; 2) Men; and General
  Response to Questionnaire

Women (Form 1)

1) *Age* (in completed years): under 15; 15-24; 25-34; 35-44;
   45-54; 55-64; over 64

2) *Place of birth*: Urban; Urban slum; Village; Nomad

3) *Present Residence*: Urban; Urban slum; Village; Nomad

4) *How long have you lived here?* (years): under 5; 5-10; over 10

5) *What is your tribe?*

6) *What is your religion?* Muslim; Christian, Other

7) *Education* (completed years): Illiterate; Khalwa (home
   education); 1-6 years; 7-9; 10; 12; over 12; Don't know

8) *Education of mother*: Illiterate; Khalwa; Elementary; Intermediate; Secondary; post-Secondary; Don't know

9) *Education of father*: (as above)

10) *Education of husband*: (as above)

11) *Occupation*: of Respondent; of Father; of Mother; of
    Husband

12) *Income per year*: (Sudanese £s) of Respondent; of Father;
    of Mother; of Husband; specify for each if: under 400;
    400-1,200; over 1,200

13) *Present marital status*: Single; Engaged; Married; Divorced;
    Widowed; Other

14) *Age at first menstrual cycle*: under 9 years; 10; 11; 12; 13;
    14; 15; 16 or more; Don't know

15) *Is your menstrual cycle*: Regular; Painful

16) *Is circumcision practiced amongst female members of your
    family?* Yes; No; Don't know

17) *Is your mother/elder sister(s)/younger sister(s) circumcised?*
    No; Yes/Type: Sunna/Pharaonic/Intermediate/Don't know;
    Don't know whether circumcised

18) *Are your daughters circumcised?* No daughters; daughters not
    old enough; elder daughters are; all are; daughters old
    enough but uncircumcised; Don't know

19) *If daughters circumcised, which type?* Sunna; Pharaonic; Intermediate; All different types; Don't know

(If uncircumcised, please ignore questions 20 to 34)

20) *At what age were you circumcised?*
21) *Where were you circumcised?*
22) *What was the type of circumcision?*
23) *By whom was it performed?*
24) *Was anaesthesia used?*
25) *What instrument(s) was used?*
26) *Were you given tablets, or injections?*
27) *Were you given native medicine?*
28) *Was any local medicine traditionally used?*   Specify or
29) *How was the wound approximated?*   state if
30) *How long did it take to heal?*   not known
31) *Did you suffer any complications as a result?* If yes, specify
32) *Did you need medical treatment?*
33) *If you suffered complications what happened to the operator?*
34) *Have you ever been decircumcised (deinfibulated)?* If yes, specify reason; state how many times

(If unmarried please ignore questions 35 to 48)

35) *Before marriage was your menstrual cycle regular? Did you experience painful menstrual cycles?*
36) *Was your marriage arranged with your consent?*
37) *How long have you been married?*
38) *How many pregnancies?*
39) *How many children living?*
40) *Do either you or your husband use any method of contraception?*
41) *How soon after marriage were you pregnant?*
42) *Were you afraid of your first sexual intercourse?* If yes, state reason
43) *Did tears and bleeding follow?*
44) *How long before your husband achieved complete penetration?*
45) *Did your husband experience difficulty in this respect?* If yes, state methods attempted to remedy the situation
46) *If you have been recircumcised (reinfibulated) state:* When; How often; If you wanted it; Who did it; Where your most recent recircumcision took place; Why you undertook to

have it done; If any complication followed; If your
husband wanted it

47) *How was your first delivery conducted?*

48) *Did you experience complications with your first delivery?*
If yes, specify what happened to the foetus

49) *Have you ever suffered from any of the following?* Keloid at
site of circumcision; vulvar abscesses; inclusion cysts;
recurrent urinary tract infection; chronic pelvic infection;
difficult or impossible sexual penetration; pain during
intercourse; difficulty in passing menses; infertility; vaginal
deposits/stones; nervous troubles; none of these; others,
specify; don't know

50) *Do you think that female circumcision should continue?*
If yes, state type; state reasons for saying 'yes'. If No,
state why and give opinion on best way to abolish the
practice, specify how this could be done.

51) *State economic status of family*: Lower class; Lower middle;
Upper middle; Upper

(For circumcised respondents)

52) *Do (did) you want to be circumcised?*

53) *What was your feeling when the operation was about to be
performed?*

54) *Was the occasion celebrated?* If yes, did you receive new
clothes, gertig, etc; specify

55) *Were you circumcised alone or with a group?*

56) *Do you know of any complications to other family members
due to circumcision? or deaths due to this cause?* If yes,
specify

(For single or betrothed women)

57) *How do you think of sexual intercourse in your future
marriage?* Specify

(For married or ex-married respondents)

58) *What is the usual form for your sexual intercourse?* Vaginal;
Anal; Other; Unwilling to answer

59) *If not vaginal, why?* If willing to answer, specify

60) *What is your feeling about sexual relations with your
husband?* Pleasure; indifference; distaste; fear; unwilling
to answer

61) *Do you achieve sexual satisfaction (orgasm)?*

62) *Do you suffer nervous tension during intercourse?* If yes,
is this related to circumcision?

63) *Do you discuss circumcision of your daughters with*: no one;

husband; mother/sisters/mother-in-law; father/father-in-law; neighbours/friends; all; others, specify

64) *Which of those relatives/friends favour circumcision?*
65) *Do you plan to have all your daughters/future daughters circumcised?* If yes, specify type

(For respondents who oppose circumcision)

66) *Have you shared in any activities for abolishing this practice?* If yes, specify
67) *Why do you think this practice continues?*

(Physical examination of those willing to ascertain: *Type of circumcision*; and *Evidence of complications*)

Men (Form 2)

(Questions 1-13 and 65-67 as for women's questionnaire)

14) *Is circumcision practiced amongst female members of your immediate family?*

15) *Is your mother/elder sister(s)/younger sister(s) circumcised?* If yes, specify which, and type performed

(If unmarried ignore questions 16 to 26)

16) *Is your wife circumcised?* If yes, specify type

17) *Are your daughters circumcised?* If yes, state type(s)

18) *What action, if any, did you take in the circumcision of your daughters?* Specify

19) *Did you consent to the arrangement of your marriage?*

20) *How long have you been married?*

21) *How many children do you have?*

22) *Do you or your wife employ any contraceptive method?*

23) *Were you afraid of your first sexual intercourse?* If yes, state why

24) *How long before you achieved full penetration?*

25) *Did you find difficulties in this respect?* If yes, state how you attempted to overcome them

26) *Does your wife have recircumcision (reinfibulation)?* If yes, do you agree that it should be done?

27) *Do you consider that female circumcision should continue?* If yes, specify type and reasons for saying 'yes'. If no, state why and give opinion on best way to abolish the practice, specify how this could be done

(Unmarried respondents ignore questions 28 to 31)

28) *If divorced, was this related to circumcision?* If yes, specify

29) *What is the usual form for your sexual intercourse?* If willing, specify and give reasons

30) *Do you and your wife experience sexual pleasure*: equally/ do you enjoy it more/less than her; does she enjoy it more/ less than you?

31) *Do you always achieve sexual satisfaction (orgasm)?*

32) *How do you anticipate your first sexual intercourse?* With pleasure/fear/don't know/unwilling to answer.

General Response to Questionnaire

Generally, the response to the questionnaire was very good. That for women was 3,210 out of 3,397 (94.7%) and for men, 1,545 out of 1,699 (94.7%). 95% of the women answered both sections of the questionnaire, but only 12 agreed to be examined. 94.6% of the men answered both sections. The women were more frank in their answers.

There were no difficulties in introducing the subject or obtaining information from rural people. Dealing with urban people was, on the contrary, more difficult; and some of them refused to answer and were generally uncooperative.

Communication with the sheikh or the community leader, explaining to him the purpose of the research, emphasizing its academic nature and disclaiming any association with governmental bodies, helped a great deal in getting a favourable level of response. This co-operation was very important, otherwise people may have refused to answer, or have given false information. To facilitate our work, the sheikh usually asked some young people to accompany us during the home visits.

For several reasons coverage of the survey was least in Eastern Sudan. There was the problem of language; translation into local dialects was sometimes difficult. Secondly, traditionally it is unacceptable for a stranger to enter their houses, let alone talk about this sensitive subject. Thirdly, before a woman can speak, she must obtain the permission of her husband or father; this was often refused. Sometimes the husband insisted on attending the interview and answering instead of his wife. Those women who dared speak said that to speak of sex is shameful and considered it an insult. The men were more difficult than women.

All the midwives were helpful, except for two from Northern Darfur who denied ever having performed the operation.

In some remote villages, the question of whether or not circumcision was practiced in their families caused astonishment and laughter among the women. Some could not believe that there were other 'real women' who had not been circumcised. Each one had a story to tell about a sister or a friend who had died as a result of consequences of the practice, but none of them had considered the possibility of its elimination or questioned its value. For these reasons talking about this subject, especially if one wants to get useful information, is really a difficult experience. Nevertheless the information and results obtained were satisfactory.

Table A1
Respondents by Age

Age Group (years)	Female		Male	
	No.	%	No.	%
Under 15	64	2	–	–
15-24	1,271	39.6	299	19.35
25-34	941	29.3	453	29.3
35-44	565	17.6	394	25.5
45-54	234	7.3	226	14.6
55-64	84	2.6	123	8
Over 64	51	1.6	50	3.2
Total	*3,210*	*100*	*1,545*	*100*

Note: All men were over 15 years

Table A2
Educational Level: Female Respondents, Their Mothers,
Fathers and Husbands; and of Male Respondents

Education	Respondent	Mother	Father	Husband	Male Resp.
Illiterate	1,390	2,697	1,358	435	396
Khalwa	99	87	944	386	229
Elementary	918	225	446	481	373
Intermediate	395	80	238	330	174
Secondary	331	22	99	316	242
Post-secondary	77	3	80	233	131
Do not know	–	96	45	95	–
Total	*3,210*	*3,210*	*3,210*	*2,276*	*1,545*

Table A3
Occupations: of Female Respondents, Their Mothers,
Fathers and Husbands; and of Male Respondents

Occupation	Female Respondent	Mother	Father	Husband	Male Respondent
Trading	68	195	528	376	209
Farmers	564	665	834	571	220
Skilled workers	90	71	288	215	418
Unskilled workers	42	—	306	301	186
Clerical	75	7	54	84	164
Semi-professionals	72	25	60	135	49
Professionals	25	2	48	85	111
No occupation	1,180	744	1,074	178	68
Housewives	1,692	1,475	—	—	—
Students	402	—	—	2	101
Others	—	—	36	11	19
Total	*3,210*	*3,210*	*3,210*	*1,958*	*1,545*

Table A4
Respondents by Marital Status

	Female	Male
Single	818	453
Engaged	116	47
Married	1,958	11
Divorced	116	21
Widowed	170	—
Other	32	13
Total	*3,210*	*1,545*

Northern Sudan

1) Halfawyeen
2) Danagla
3) Mahas
    Hardokab
    Burhat
    Subhab
    Dakhlab
    Onab
    Miknab
    Khoglab
    Wawisi
    Jana El Hag
    Awlad Falata
    Awlad Mania
4) Shaygia
5) Jaalyeen
    Manaseer
    Rubatab
    Mirfab
    Fadlab
    Dodab
    Hakinab
    Magidia
    Kirtan
6) Fadnia
7) Abdallab
8) Batahin
9) Shukria
10) Kenana
11) Hassania
12) Halaween
13) Shanabla
14) Ahamda
15) Beni Salim

16) Rufaa Sharg
    Lahaween
    Beni Omran
    Awamra
    Dabaseen
    Zabania
17) Rufaa El Hewai
    Dar Hamid
    Beni Jerar
    Zyadia
    Pazar
    Maalia
    Maakla
    Dwahia
    Maslamia

Western Sudan

18) Baggara
    Tasisha
    Rizeigat
    Beni Hilba
    Mahria
    Humur
    Messirriya
    Hawazma
    Hatia
    Takia
    Tirgam
    Beni Khuzam
    Beni Hussein
    Beni Zayad
19) Kababish

Magarba
20) Hwaweer
    Gallaba (Hawara)
    Wahiya
    Koriat
21) Berti
22) Dago
23) Fur
24) Zaghawa
25) Midob
26) Barno
27) Hausa
28) Masalit
29) Beni Hussein
30) Nuba
31) Kardis
32) Bediriya
33) Jawama
34) Rikabia
35) Ababda

Eastern Sudan

36) Beni Amir
37) Hadendwa
38) Amrar
39) Bushareen
40) Shirab

41) Rashaida
42) Mawalid
43) Kawahla
44) El Ingessana
45) El Broon
    El Awduk
    El Gamgum
    Sban
46) Gumuz
47) Funj
48) Wataweet
49) Barta
50) Fazugli

Southern Sudan

51) Dinka
52) Nuer
53) Shilluk
54) Zandi
55) Tabusa
56) Latuka
57) Bari
58) Mandaria
59) Ashuli
60) Moro
61) Murle
62) El Anwak

120

Circumcision

Countries where circumcision is practiced include:

Africa: almost all countries.
Asia: Malaysia, Indonesia, Southern parts of the Arab Peninsula and along the Persian Gulf, Pakistan, Russia (some sects), United Arab Emirates, Oman, Bahrein and South Yemen (Worsley, 1938; Schaefer, 1955; Hathout, 1963).
South America: Peru, Brazil and Eastern Mexico.
Australia: from Urabunna in the South, throughout the continent, to the Eastern shores of the Gulf of Carpentaria. The Pitta-Patta practise introcision (Worsley, 1938).

In Africa, where it is most widely distributed, different types are practiced for various reasons among different religious and ethnic groups.

Infibulation
This is practiced in: Sudan, Somalia, Djibouti, Eritria, Egypt, northern Kenya, northern Nigeria, Mali, and Central African Republic.

Excision
This is practiced in: Chad, Central African Republic, Nigeria, Zaire, Ghana, Togo, Benin, Ivory Coast, Mali, Upper Volta, Senegal, Gambia, Sierra Leone, Mauritania, Kenya, Tanzania and Ethiopia.

Sunna
This type is practiced in Sudan and Egypt.

1) Trained midwives

B.A., 35 years old from Gezira, was the only sister-midwife I met
who did circumcision. She was the famous sister-midwife of whom
I had heard and who did most of the circumcisions in Medani.

I visited her in the early evening, and shortly after I arrived a
group of women brought two little girls — three and five years
old — for circumcision. I asked if I might attend the operation
and this was agreed.

The girls' aunt said that their fathers had requested the sunna
type, but the other women objected, saying this was not men's
business, and asked for the pharaonic type. B.A. said that she
would comply with the fathers' wishes.

A plastic mat was laid over the bed and the first little girl was
held in position by her relatives. The operator then prepared
herself, washing her hands first with soap and water and then
with disinfectant. She washed the child's genital area with disinfectant before performing the operation. The little girl cried and
screamed and her relatives tried to calm her, saying it was only a
very small operation and that when it was done she would be a big
girl, and so on.

Interestingly, the type performed was not sunna, but one degree
of the intermediate type. When I commented on this the midwife
insisted that it *was* sunna. What she actually did was to clasp the
clitoris and labia minora with the forceps, cut, and then stitch the
two sides together. She said she stitched the wound mainly to
prevent bleeding.

She performed the same operation on the other child who was
much more afraid than the younger girl had been, even though she
had not been present during the operation. She totally refused
circumcision, but her relatives held her down forcibly for the
operation.

When the women and children had left we continued our discussion. B.A. said she had not been taught how to circumcise but
had learned after her midwifery training. She had become
interested in circumcision whilst working in the obstetrics and
gynaecological ward of the Medani Hospital, where she had seen
cases which had resulted in complications.

Her first circumcision was carried out in 1971, when a woman came saying that although her niece had died of tetanus after circumcision there was no way not to have her daughter circumcised, and had asked her to do this. She agreed, and circumcised the girl with the intermediate type and has continued to perform this type since. It is better, in her opinion, because the area is covered and thus infection of the genital area is prevented, as little girls often play naked on the ground. Although she considered the intermediate to be sunna, she never performed the pharaonic type. She had no fears about performing circumcision because all the 'important people' in her area brought their girls to her to be circumcised. The operation was usually carried out at her home in the late afternoon or early evening. Many cases were brought to her from nearby villages, because her circumcision was judged to be good and hygienic. She did not consider this part of her work as a major source of income; the rate was (Sudanese) £5-10 per case, though she is sometimes given more, according to the financial means of her clients. In the season, she can perform up to 15-20 operations daily, but at other times there are only two or three each day.

Before I began to question her about complications two ladies came into the house and waited in another room. I guessed they had come for recircumcision (reinfibulation), but the midwife said they were friends who had come to visit and they would wait.

She admitted that she had, occasionally, had some complications — such as slight bleeding and urine retention, but never any case of infection. She told me of three cases she would always remember because they had been very difficult experiences. Two of them were cardiac cases, and the third a case of thrombocytopenia. In the first case, she told me, five women and a girl of about ten years of age came to her. They said the girl was subject to fainting attacks and was a suspected cardiac case. Other midwives had refused to circumcise her, and B.A. also advised them not to have her circumcised, but they insisted. Eventually, on condition that they stayed the whole day: 'I agreed to the operation. I used a local anaesthetic with adrenaline and — thanks to God — nothing happened to her.' The other cardiac case had been referred to her by a paediatrician, who had told the girl's relatives they must stay at least one day at the operator's house. The girl was 13 years old and her relatives were ashamed that she was so old and still not circumcised. The same procedure was followed for her and the operation went off without complications.

The third case involved a nine year old girl whose relatives told B.A. that ever since she was small she had bled profusely, even from a very superficial wound. 'I thought this was a case of purpura, and advised them against having the child circumcised, but they insisted, because it was shameful if she was not. I agreed to risk the operation and prepared vitamin K injections and calcium and asked the child's relatives to stay that day with me.' The operation appeared to be successful and they left safely. 'All

that evening I was worried about the case' B.A. said. 'The
following day, just as I had feared, the girl was carried to me with
severe bleeding. After examination I realized this was venous
blood and so I applied compressions and the bleeding stopped —
thanks to God.' Her relatives said the bleeding had started during
the night. They had not taken her to hospital because they were
afraid they would be asked about the operator. 'But I told them
they could have taken her, because all the staff know that I do
circumcision and not only send cases to me for the operation, but
help by giving me anaesthesia and equipment.'

She then excused herself to see her visitors. On her return, very
suddenly I asked her if they had come for recircumcision. She
admitted that they had, and this led to a discussion on the
subject. She performs this operation only on request usually, but
sometimes does it because she considers it necessary, for example,
when the skin becomes very loose after several deliveries.

She said, too, that from her experience there are girls who do
not really need to be circumcised because their genitalia is very
small, but in other cases circumcision is essential.

In another interview with a trained midwife — M.A. — from a
village near Sennar, she told me she had been working for 16
years following graduation from the Medani Midwifery School.
She said, 'That to be a midwife in the past was considered shameful. When I was chosen for training everyone said that I would be
a prostitute. This angered my mother and caused my brother to
become a psychiatric case. Until they were convinced of what the
work really entailed I had a hard time.'

She said she usually performed pharaonic circumcision because
this was requested, but that she preferred the sunna, as this type
had been recommended when she was in training. I asked what she
meant by sunna, and she explained that after injecting a local
anaesthesia she takes only the clitoris, or sometimes parts from the
sides, and occasionally stitches to prevent bleeding. She said
nobody asked for sunna in her area, but that everyone wanted the
pharaonic type. Even some girls were taken to her who had
already been sunna circumcised, or whose circumcision was not
good, for her to circumcise again satisfactorily.

I asked if there were no midwives in Sennar. She said that there
were, but their circumcision was not good because they used
scissors and consequently cut a lot of tissue and this resulted in
failure of the wound to heal. 'I use razors for circumcision and
recircumcision [reinfibulation] and scissors only for delivery', she
told me. She explained that a wound made by scissors will not
heal because it is thin and that any slight movement will cause it
to open; similarly if the girl retains urine or coughs, or has an itch.

She told me that women also went to her for recircumcision
even if they have been delivered in other areas. Her circumcision
and recircumcision were said to be good and that of other midwives was not. Apparently all the other midwives were jealous of

her; some complained to the doctors and had even tried to attack her. One doctor told a complaining midwife that he could do nothing to prevent M.A. circumcising, because people went to her — she did not go to them.

At this point, the lady who had accompanied me joined the discussion and said, 'What M. says is right. There are some midwives who take all the tissue and leave only bone, and sometimes take up to two hours doing the operation. I know of a girl in another village who was staying with her aunt who had not had her circumcised. The girl was engaged and went to her mother asking her what she should do as her marriage was near.' They called in an untrained midwife to perform the operation and on the second day afterwards her father's sister was teasing her and hit her on the thigh and, 'As a result the circumcision wound opened and gaped like a donkey's mouth.' The girl was then taken to a trained midwife but the wound failed to heal. When she was married she told her husband about it, and said that if he did not want her he should leave her and she would return his money. He did, in fact, divorce the girl. The wound could not be stitched because all the tissue had been taken so there was no flesh left to heal together. 'It was left just like a bad water-melon.' 'Oh God', I said, 'that means she will never be married?' and the woman replied, 'Of course. Men will not marry an uncircumcised woman, and in her state the girl is considered to be uncircumcised. We hear that the men said so when they were talking together.' I asked her, if her husband had wanted circumcision, 'Naturally', she answered, 'No man refuses it for a woman, because this is how we live.'

I went on to ask M.A. if she had ever had any complications during her work. She said 'Never', and that usually she administered antibiotics. As far as her fee was concerned she told me that in her own area she accepts whatever is offered — £2-3. For cases brought to her from other areas it is £5, if she goes to them she is paid £10. For deliveries £5-10, and for recircumcision £5 if the woman went to her and £10 if a man took her to the woman. 'I used to circumcise between three and seven cases daily. I prefer to do the operation in the evening, because it is calm and the girl will sleep peacefully and waken without crying or bleeding. I use razors, one for each case, because I am afraid of tetanus. I never take the government kit out with me to circumcision, because there may be an unexpected check on them, and we are forbidden to use the government's equipment for circumcision.'

2) Untrained midwives

Because adults would refuse to tell me the whereabouts of any untrained midwife I had to ask small children to take me to them; in that way they were in no position to deny that they were midwives. Some said to me that in the past they had been midwives but not any longer; some were unafraid and admitted that they still worked, but often their daughters or sisters would intervene to say that, in fact, they no longer worked as midwives, or would warn her that perhaps I was from the government, and sometimes even forbade the woman to talk to me at all. A few did, however, talk frankly to me.

For example, T.H., aged 45 years from El Kiriba village close to Medani told me that she had been working for 17 years. Her father and other members of the family were *basirs* (people who reduce fractures) and she had started to deliver when a relative was in labour and no midwife could be found. Her father had compelled her to deliver the women, and though she was hesitant she managed it. From that time she had assisted deliveries and performed circumcision. From using knives for circumcision she now used razors or scissors and had learned how to stitch and administer anaesthesia. She said she now has more cases than the trained midwife, because she accepts whatever is offered by way of fees, and has no specific charge; she sometimes charges nothing at all.

She usually did pharaonic circumcision because only the Barno and Fallata asked for sunna; the men in her area preferred the pharaonic type. She told me that sometimes she stitches the wound and sometimes not, according to the wishes of the relatives. For unstitched cases the wound is washed with Dettol and the girl's legs bound together for seven days.

She went on, 'I learned to recircumcise, [reinfibulate] using stitching, so well that women from other villages are brought to me for this; they usually pay me £2-3. I have done a lot of decircumcision [deinfibulation] too, especially for new brides. I use scissors for this.'

She said that whenever she is faced with a complicated case in delivery she immediately took the woman to hospital. For complications arising from circumcision she tried to treat them herself, but if she failed took them to hospital. When I commented on this she corrected herself and said that in case of circumcision complications she instructed the girl's relatives to take her to hospital, because she is quite sure no one would reveal her name.

She would like to be trained because she already knows how to deliver, and training would help her to do her work better.

I also met H.K. who was a very old, (85 years) blind woman in a village not far south of Sennar. She no longer works, but her daughter, who inherited her job, said that she did a few deliveries, especially when a trained midwife could not be found. She said that she had delivered a case only two weeks ago, because after a pause she said, 'The woman was suspected of being a lepromatous case and her relatives asked me to help, but after that my son has prevented me from doing any more deliveries.'

I was told that neither mother or daughter had ever performed circumcision operations, neither had they attended such operations and did not know how to perform them. As members of the Ansar sect (followers of Mahdi) they were taught that circumcision is contrary to the teaching of Islam — especially the pharaonic type; but they had taken their daughter to other mid-wives for circumcision — presumably with the sunna type. Knowing nothing of the performance of circumcision operations they likewise knew nothing about recircumcision.

Bibliography

Abu Shama, A.O. et al. (1949) 'Female Circumcision in the
Sudan'. *Lancet*, 1:545.
Baasher, T.A. (1977) 'Psychological Aspects of Female Circum-
cision'. Contribution to the 5th Sudanese Congress of Obstetrics
and Gynaeocology, Khartoum, Sudan, 4-8 February 1977.
WHO/EMRO/Technical Publication No. 2, Alexandria.
Central Record Office (Sudan) Civsec Medical, File No. 44, B.2.1.
Central Record Office (Sudan), Dakhlia, Files No. (1) 44/1/3;
(1) 44/1/4; (1) 44/2/5; (1) 44/2/6.
Cook, R. (1979) 'Damage to Physical Health from Pharaonic Cir-
cumcision (Infibulation) of Females. A review of medical litera-
ture'. WHO/EMRO/Technical Publication No. 2, Alexandria.
Diallo, A. (1977/78) 'L'excision en Milieu Bambarel'. Thesis of the
Ecole Normale Superieure de Bamako, Mali. (Trans. Fran P.
Hosken, Women's International Network News, 4, No. 3.
Summer 1978).
El Dareer, A.A. (1979) 'Female Circumcision and its Consequences
for Mother and Child'. Contribution to the ILO African Sympo-
sium on the World of Work and the Protection of the Child.
Yaounde, Cameroon, 12-15 December, 1979.
Hall, L. (1963) 'Arthritis after Female Circumcision'. *East African
Medical Journal*, 40:55-7.
Hansen, H.H. (1972/73) 'Clitoridectomy: Female Circumcision in
Egypt'. *Folk*, 14-15:15-26.
Hathout, H.M. (1963) 'Some Aspects of Female Circumcision'.
Journal of Obstetrics and Gynaecology of the British Empire,
80, pp:505-7.
Hosken, F.P. (1979) 'The Hosken Report, Genital and Sexual
Mutilation of Females'. Women's International Network.
Lexington, U.S.A.
Huber, A. (1969) 'Die Weiblivhe Beschneidung', *Zeitschrift fur
Tropennedizin und Parasitologie*, 20:1-9. (Trans. German
Embassy, Sudan, 1978).
Huddleston, C.E. (1949) 'Female Circumcision in the Sudan'.
Lancet, 1:626.
Karim, M. and Ammar, R. (1965) *Female Circumcision and
Sexual Desire*. Ain Shams University Press, Cairo, Egypt.
Kennedy, J.G. (1970) 'Circumcision and Excision in Egyptian

Nubia'. *Man*, London, New Series, 5, No. 2:175-91.

Kenyatta, J. (1965) *Facing Mount Kenya*. Vintage Books, a
Division of Random House, New York.

Laycock, H.T. (1950) 'Surgical Aspects of Female Circumcision
in Somali Land'. *East African Medical Journal*, 27:445-50.

Lenzi, E. (1970) 'Damage Caused by Infibulation and Infertility'.
Acta Europaea Fortilitatis, 2:47-58.

MacDonald, D.R. (1948) 'Female Circumcision' (Central Record
Office, Sudan), Civsec Medical, File No. 44, B.2.1.

Melly, J.M. (1935) 'Infibulation'. *Lancet*, 2:1272.

Modawi, S. (1974) 'The Impact of Social and Economic Changes
in Female Circumcision'. Proceedings of the Third Congress
of Obstetrics and Gynaecology, Khartoum, April, 1973, Sudan
Medical Association Congress Series No. 1:242-54.

————— (1977) 'Changing Aspects of Circumcision in the
Sudan'. Contribution to the 5th Congress of Obstetrics and
Gynaecology, Khartoum, Sudan. 14-18 February 1977.
(Pamphlet).

Montagu, A. (1946) 'Ritual Mutilation Among Primitive Peoples'.
Ciba Symposium, Ciba Pharmaceutical Products, Inc., New
Jersey, 8, No. 8:421-36.

Mustafa, A.Z. (1966) 'Female Circumcision and Infibulation'.
Journal of Obstetrics and Gynaecology. British Commonwealth,
April, 73:302-06.

Ploss, H. and Bartels, M. (eds.) (1895) *Das Wieb in der Natur und
Volkerkunde*. Trans. and edited by Eric John Dingwall.
(Heinemann Medical Books Ltd. London, 1935).

Pridie, E.D., et al. (1951) 'Female Circumcision in the Anglo-
Egyptian Sudan'. Sudan Government Publication (McC 285)
S.G. 1185 C.S. 5000 6/51.

Remondino, P.C. (1891) *History of Circumcision from the Earliest
Times to the Present*. F.A. Davis Co., Philadelphia.

Ryad, H. et al. (No date) 'Sukan El Sudan', (Arabic) 'People of
Sudan'. Trans. from *Republic of Sudan — Regional Geography*
by K.M. Barber, Dar El Thakafa, Beirut and Nahda Sudanese
Bookshop, Khartoum.

Schaefer, G. (1955) 'Female Circumcision'. *Journal of Obstetrics
and Gynaecology*, 6:235-8.

Seligman, C.G. and Seligman, B.Z. (1965) *Pagan Tribes of the
Nilotic Sudan*. London, Routledge and K. Paul.

Sequeira, J.H. (1931) 'Female Circumcision and Infibulation',
Lancet, 2:1054-56.

Shandall, Ahmed Abu El Futuh (1967) 'Circumcision and Infibulation of Females. A general Consideration of the Problem and
a Clinical Study of the Complications in Sudanese Women.'
Sudan Medical Journal, 5:178-212.

Sheikh Ahmed El Tahir (1945) In *Female Circumcision in the
Anglo-Egyptian Sudan*. A pamphlet issued by Sudan Medical
Service. Edited by Pridie and MacDonald, Khartoum.

Taba, A.H. (1979) 'Female Circumcision' in *Traditional Practices*

Affecting the Health of Women and Children. WHO/EMRO Technical Publication No.2, Alexandria.

Thiam, A. (1978) *La Parole aux Negresses*. Donoel/Gonthier, Paris. (Translated and reviewed by F.P. Hosken. Hosken Report 1979).

Verzin, J.A. (1975) 'Sequale of Female Circumcision', *Tropical Doctor*, 5:163-9.

Widstrand, Carl Gosta (1964) 'Female Infibulation', *Studia Ethnographica Upsaliensa*, 20:95-6.

World Health Organization (1979) Seminar Report on 'Traditional practices affecting the Health of Women and Children'. 10-15 February, Khartoum, Sudan. WHO/EMRO/Technical Publiccation No. 2, Alexandria.

Worsley, A. (1938) 'Infibulation and Female Circumcision: A study of a Littleknown Custom'. *Journal of Obstetrics and Gynaecology of the British Empire*, 45:686-91.

Other Books Available from Zed Press

On Women

Ingela Bendt and Jim Downing
We Shall Return: Women of Palestine
Hb and Pb

Patricia Jeffery
Frogs in a Well
Indian Women in Purdah
Hb and Pb

Bonnie Mass
Population Target
The Political Economy of Population Control in Latin America
Hb and Pb

Maria Mies
The Lace Makers of Narsapur
Indian Housewives and the World Market
Pb

Christine Obbo
African Women
Their Struggles for Independence
Hb and Pb

Gail Omvedt
We Shall Smash This Prison!
Indian Women in Struggle
Hb and Pb

Margaret Randall
Sandino's Daughters
Testimonies of Nicaraguan Women in Struggle
Pb

Else Skjonsberg
A Special Caste?
Tamil Village Women in Sri Lanka Today
Hb

Agnes Smedley
Portraits of Chinese Women
Pb

Zed Press titles cover Africa, Asia, Latin America and the Middle East, as well as general issues affecting the Third World's relations with the rest of the world. Our Series embrace Imperialism, Women, Political Economy, History, Labour, Voices of Struggle, Human Rights and other areas pertinent to the Third World.

You can order Zed titles direct from Zed Press, 57 Caledonian Road, London N1 9DN, U.K.